T.D. JAKES

SIX PILLARS FROM EPHESIANS

Celebrating Marriage

THE SPIRITUAL WEDDING OF THE BELIEVER

ALBURY PUBLISHING
Tulsa, Oklahoma

2nd Printing

Six Pillars From Ephesians: Celebrating Marriage
The Spiritual Wedding of the Believer
ISBN 1-57778-110-4
Copyright © 2000 by T. D. Jakes
T. D. Jakes Ministries
International Communications Center
P. O. Box 210887
Dallas, Texas 75211

Published by ALBURY PUBLISHING
P. O. Box 470406
Tulsa, Oklahoma 74147-0406

CONTENTS

☙

CELEBRATING MARRIAGE
THE SPIRITUAL WEDDING OF THE BELIEVER

©

INTRODUCTION

Everybody loves a wedding! A wedding is considered great cause for celebration, not only by the bride and groom, but by family members, friends, and even those who don't know the happy couple. When a man and woman pledge their entire lives to one another, it is one of the most sacred and cherished moments for them and for all who stand with them. They are making vows of fidelity and love to each other for life.

We all know the love story of the ages: Man and woman meet, they fall in love, they marry, and they live happily ever after. But we always must remember that weddings are God's idea. From the beginning, God anticipated that man and woman would be joined together in a holy union, a holy mating, or holy matrimony. He called this sacred covenant becoming *one flesh* (see Genesis 2:24), and this joining in marriage became His most vibrant illustration to fallen mankind of the intimate relationship He sought with them.

Why did God choose to describe His love relationship and lasting commitment to a union with His people through the experience and significance of a wedding and a marriage? Throughout the Old Testament we find references to God being the bridegroom of His people, who are His bride:

> As the bridegroom rejoiceth over the bride, so shall thy God rejoice over thee.
>
> ISAIAH 62:5

In the New Testament, the Holy Spirit gives us the crowning joy of the mystery. Jesus, our Savior and Lord, is the bridegroom of the Church, and we are His beloved bride:

> There came unto me one of the seven angels...and talked with me, saying, Come hither, I will shew thee the bride, the Lamb's wife.
>
> REVELATION 21:9

The apostle Paul gracefully addressed this issue in writing to the Ephesians. His teaching on this subject in the epistles is one of the most beautiful and yet practical about how we are wedded to the Lord Jesus Christ. This teaching is at the very heart of what it means to be loved and cherished by God and to be one with Him.

I believe God chose the wedding and marriage to illustrate His relationship with His people because it is the most intimate and personal relationship we experience in our natural lives. And when our hearts and minds begin to see and understand the depths and richness of this revelation — we are forever loved by and married to Jesus Christ — the ecstasy of our position and condition in Him is beyond expression!

1

OUR KINSMAN REDEEMER

In the book of Ruth, God gives us a beautiful example of how Jesus becomes our Bridegroom and we become His beloved. As a Moabitess and former idol worshipper, Ruth represents the Church. Like her, we once lived under the rule and influence of Satan and a world system that is totally opposed to God's kingdom. As Ruth's deliverer, Boaz represents Jesus. Jesus is our kinsman in the flesh who loves us, pays the price to redeem us from our spiritual poverty, and then takes us as His bride. Throughout the Bible, God repeatedly uses weddings and marriage to reveal to us His pursuit of us, His love for us, and His desire to be with us forever.

Marriage is a God-created relationship.

In spite of what many people think, marriage has never been a secular institution. In fact, those who follow the dictates of the world, the lusts of their flesh, and the lies of the enemy have very little use for marriage. They would just as soon be single so they can fornicate and commit adultery with whomever they choose. It doesn't bother them to father children and never be a father to those children. It doesn't bother them to have children by several different fathers and never have contact with those fathers again. The world has little regard for the demands of fidelity and "until death do us part" vows, and they have a high degree of tolerance for marital infidelity, separation, and divorce.

However, marriage is holy and divine in its very definition and nature. That's because God created the wedding and marriage to be a picture of how Jesus would pursue, commit to, and love His bride and how His bride should love and cherish Him in return. When a man and woman come together at a wedding, it is a sacred, spiritual act. Where the world views marriage as a partnership, like a merger between two companies, the Church views marriage as the divine, sacred reuniting of *Adam*, the first human who was both male and female.

> *Therefore shall a man leave his father and his mother, and shall cleave unto his wife: and they shall be one flesh.*
>
> GENESIS 2:24

In marriage, male and female are re-fused and re-bonded into one flesh. Furthermore, what God reveals about Adam and Eve — and about the relation-ship between a husband and wife — illustrates what the Church is ultimately to be to Jesus. Paul speaks of this sacred relationship to the Ephesians:

> **T**his is a great mystery: but I speak concerning Christ and the church.
>
> EPHESIANS 5:32

Although Paul writes only ten verses about marriage between husband and wife in this epistle, those verses are so rich that an entire marriage seminar could be taught out of them. And when we finish studying Ephesians 5:22 to 5:31, teaching about wives submitting to their husbands and husbands loving and cherishing and nourishing their wives, we come face to face with the reality of our marriage to the Lamb. Ultimately, natural marriage is an illustration Paul uses to show the depth of our relationship with the Lord.

There are those who call the Church the "body" of Christ, and there are those who call the Church the "bride" of Christ. Some modern teachers have argued over which is correct. They say, "If the Church is His body, which is male, it cannot be His bride, which is female." The fact is, in the first marriage between Adam and Eve, Eve was both Adam's body and his bride. She was bone of his bone and flesh of his flesh, yet she was separate from him in form and inseparably bound to him in spirit. As believers in Christ Jesus, we are inseparably bound and eternally married to the Lord Jesus Christ in spirit. Yet on this earth, we live out His life in our flesh. We are body and bride simultaneously.

ADAM AND EVE

In order to understand more fully what Paul is teaching the Ephesians and us, let's take a look at the marriage of Adam and Eve. The first man, Adam, was created in the likeness and the image of God. He was the picture God wanted to display of Himself on the earth in fleshly form.

Now Adam did not look like God physically because God is Spirit in His essence and spirit has no form or physique. Nor did Adam look quite like me or any man alive on the earth today. Adam was a *created* man, created by God without blemish or defect. I don't have any idea how Adam looked — I wasn't there! But I know this. He was *like* his Creator. His Creator is Father God, and Adam was like God. Adam was distinctive from all other created beings. He had self-awareness, creative thought, and the ability to communicate with God in a personal way.

Male and female created he them; and blessed them, and called their name Adam, in the day when they were created.

GENESIS 5:2

God called their name Adam — male and female created He *them*. Adam was a perfect person and he had complete dominion over everything. He had a position granted to him by his Creator and an image that reflected his Creator. When Adam stood up and began to walk about this earth, he was a different person than you and I. I'm not talking about the color of his skin, the color of his hair, the features of his face, or the build of his body. He walked about this earth and had total dominion over every aspect of the earth.

How long did Adam exist in this state of wholeness and perfection in God's image? We don't know. We only know this: He was alone. Then one day God said that his state of aloneness was no longer suitable. For the first time in the act of creation, God proclaimed, "It is not good."

And the Lord God said, It is not good that the man should be alone; I will make him an help meet for him.

GENESIS 2:18

When God said, "It is not good for man to be alone," the word "alone" is the Hebrew word *badow*, which means to be by oneself, the only one. This word lends itself to the concept of being the only one of a species. To illustrate His point, God brought every living creature before Adam and he named them, including the fish of the sea, the fowl of the air, the beasts of the field, and all creeping and crawling things. In every species, Adam encountered male and female. Male and female bluebirds. Male and female dolphins. Male and female ants.

Finally, God took Adam and put him to sleep and said, "I don't have to reach down in the dirt to create anything for you, because you are so much like Me that I need only reach inside you, pull something out of you that is already in you, and use it to create a helpmeet for you."

God reached into Adam's side and out of his being He pulled out a rib and from that rib constructed a woman. I can just imagine that as Adam awoke and saw the woman he said, "She is me! She is my body, bone of my bone, flesh of my flesh, just like me except with a womb. I will call her womb-man or woman." Of course, Adam didn't actually say she was a womb-man but the observation is valid in that the distinctive difference between Adam and Eve is that Eve was given the ability to bear children. Adam knew she was of his body. He could become one with her because she came from him. And the two became one because they were one before they were two.

It is a great mystery to our minds that two can become one, and this is the mystery of the Church in its relationship to God. As human beings we have the potential to become one with God. Because God created us and gave us a portion of His nature, even in our sinfulness, we can respond to Him, be restored to Him, be reconciled to Him, be reunited with Him, and be one with Him. *One!* No longer are we man or woman separated from God, but man or woman infused with the very presence and Spirit of God. We enter into oneness with Him.

In the physical, Eve was a composite of different chromosomes, all of which were related to Adam and which could unite with his chromosomes. When Adam and Eve coupled with one another, all of Adam's masculinity and all of Eve's femininity found full expression and fulfillment and in their union multiplication and growth came forth. She was his egg; he was her sperm. When they touched each other in the fullness of their love and oneness, they were capable of producing fruit, more children for the kingdom of God — the Father's delight!

This is the mystery of Christ and the Church. It is as Jesus finds expression for His Spirit in our flesh and through our flesh — it is as we find expression in Jesus for all that we are in our souls and our spirits — that we become one with Him and together we produce the spiritual fruit of souls harvested in this earth. Hallelujah! No wonder the angels and all of heaven shout with ecstatic joy whenever another soul comes into the kingdom of God!

SATAN'S ATTACK

After we encounter the powerful yet wholly beautiful experience of becoming one both in marriage and with our Lord, is it any wonder that Satan slithered up to attack the union of Adam and Eve and continues to attack marriage today? Is it any wonder that Satan continues to attack our union with Christ Jesus? He is trying to put a stop to two things: oneness — complete union, cohesiveness, unity, bondedness — and the production of fruit!

Satan's entire effort is aimed at the overthrow of God. He gives all of his effort to the destruction of the believer's union with Christ Jesus and with other believers. He hates union and oneness and unity among believers and within the Church. Why? Because he hates the production of spiritual fruit. The last thing Satan wants is for sinners to be born again, for the oppressed to be delivered, for the demon-possessed to be set free, for new believers to grow into maturity to the full stature of Christ, for the Church to be strengthened, and for the kingdom of God to be established.

Satan is quick to slip into any group, into any union, into any marriage, into any church. And he started his attack in the Garden of Eden with the woman. He couldn't go after God because he had already done that and lost. Remember Jesus' description of that heavenly war before man was created:

> **A**nd he said unto them, I beheld Satan as lightning fall from heaven.
>
> LUKE 10:18

Therefore, when Satan attacks the Church today, He doesn't start with Jesus because he already battled Jesus and lost! He lost when he was Lucifer and rebelled against God, he lost the definitive battle at the cross and the resurrection, and he continues to lose to Jesus every time a believer takes authority over him in Jesus' name. Satan is a defeated foe, so his attacks are aimed at the believer, and his attacks on the believer ultimately target Jesus Christ. Satan isn't out to destroy us. He seeks to destroy us in order to overthrow Jesus.

When Satan came to Eve, his final destination was not Eve but Adam. Both Adam and Eve had dominion over the earth (see Genesis 1:27), but

Adam was the head. Satan intended to destroy Eve on his way to destroying Adam and as a means of gaining the earth for his own possession. The Bible tells us that before his fall, Lucifer's throne and dominion were on the earth. He is referred to as the king of Tyrus:

> **S**on of man, take up a lamentation upon the king of Tyrus, and say unto him, Thus saith the Lord God; Thou sealest up the sum, full of wisdom, and perfect in beauty.
>
> Thou hast been in Eden the garden of God; every precious stone was thy covering, the sardius, topaz, and the diamond, the beryl, the onyx, and the jasper, the sapphire, the emerald, and the carbuncle, and gold: the workmanship of thy tabrets and of thy pipes was prepared in thee in the day that thou wast created.
>
> Thou art the anointed cherub that covereth; and I have set thee so: thou wast upon the holy mountain of God; thou hast walked up and down in the midst of the stones of fire.
>
> Thou wast perfect in thy ways from the day that thou wast created, till iniquity was found in thee.
>
> EZEKIEL 28:12-15

When Adam fell and bowed his knee to Satan, Satan gained dominion over the earth again and he keeps his dominion through fallen mankind. But then Jesus, the Second Adam, did not bow His knee to Satan. And when He redeemed fallen humanity, becoming the door to the restoration of our relationship with God and our dominion on the earth, Satan's rule was threatened again.

Stop to think about this for a moment: Satan cannot destroy Jesus directly. He cannot take on the Son of God in face-to-face combat and win. But what if Satan could destroy every believer in Christ Jesus? He would not be destroying Jesus who is sitting at the right hand of the Father, but he would be destroying the manifested dominion and expression of Christ Jesus on earth. In seeking to destroy the believer, Satan's ultimate aim is to destroy the work of Christ Jesus and have the earth for himself.

If every believer was destroyed and brought into estrangement and death, and if every sinner were kept from knowing and accepting Christ Jesus as Savior, then Christ Jesus would be rendered ineffective in the earth. He would no longer have a "body" on this earth. There would be no body to give voice to the Gospel or to embrace the sinner with God's love. There would be no gifts of the Holy Spirit in operation or Bible teaching in the Church. There would be no Church!

THE SECOND ADAM

Satan's attack on Eve was intended to test the first man, Adam. After woman had partaken of the forbidden fruit, Adam looked at her as she offered the fruit to him and he came to the conclusion, "I love her so much that if she is going to die, I am going to die with her." He made the first fatal mistake. He loved the *gift* more than he loved the *Giver*.

Eve was *deceived*, but Adam *decided*. The Bible says that Adam "did eat." His decision was an act of his will. The fall of humanity didn't take place when Eve was deceived and ate. It took place when Adam deliberately and intentionally ate. The sins we commit that are born of deception do not strike at the very nature of our relationship with God. These sins are readily confessed, repented, and cast aside. But the sins we commit out of our will — as a conscious decision and plan of action — are destructive and deadly to our relationship with God. When we say, "I choose to disobey what You have said and to go my own way," we set ourselves up to receive the full wages of sin, which ultimately is separation from God and death.

It was out of Adam's decision to die with his bride that chaos broke out in the kingdom of Eden. When Adam and Eve both entered into a state of death, everything under their domain came under death. That's what a kingdom is — a domain over which you have dominion. It is what you rule and govern. When a king falls, his kingdom falls with him. When a married person falls into willful sin and chooses to become a rebel against God, what they rule is impacted. Their children suffer. Their home suffers. Their family influence in the church and community suffers.

Adam willfully chose sin and fell, so we all fell with him because we were born of his seed. We encounter this principle of the seed in the book of Hebrews:

> *Levi also, who receiveth tithes, paid tithes in Abraham. For he was yet in the loins of his father, when Melchizedec met him.*
>
> HEBREWS 7:9-10

When Abraham paid tithes, Levi paid tithes. Levi hadn't been born when Abraham paid tithes to Melchizedec; in fact, Levi was Abraham's great grandchild. But because Abraham paid tithes, the practice of paying tithes and the blessing associated with it was built into his seed, Levi. Likewise, when Adam fell, all mankind fell with him. It makes no difference what color he was or what his features were. He was flesh and blood, and when he fell, all flesh and blood fell.

The Scriptures tell us that in the fullness of time God sent forth His Son, born of a virgin. And this Son, whom we call Jesus, is the Second Adam. God places Jesus in the womb of a virgin, and He is birthed into flesh on this earth complete in Himself. Jesus is a new creation.

Then, for the joy that was set before Him, this Second Adam goes through the cross, the crown of thorns being crushed into His skull, the nails being driven into His hands and His feet, the piercing of His side, the agony of a death, taking on the sins of the world, and being forsaken by His Father. And He does it for the joy that out of His sacrifice, He is going to receive a wife — a beautiful, exquisite bride. Just as God pulled Eve out of Adam while Adam slept, after Jesus breathed His final breath on the cross, God pierced His side as a sign that His bride was being fashioned.

One man died *from* sin.

One man died *for* sin.

One man passed sin to all mankind.

One man passed righteousness to all mankind.

The first Adam died *with* his bride, but the Second Adam, Jesus Christ, died *for* His bride.

Being innocent of our sin, Jesus became our kinsman redeemer. Having come to earth as one of us, our kinsman in the flesh, He gave Himself for us, His body and His bride. Now He becomes one with us so He might have a body on this earth which will produce the glorious fruit of the Gospel: many, many children for the Father's heavenly home!

One with our Lord — this is the mystery of the Church!

2

A NEW LIFE
OF HONOR

One of the most beautiful illustrations of God's love for us is found in the Old Testament book of Hosea. God said to the prophet Hosea, "Go, take unto thee a wife of whoredoms" (Hosea 1:2). Hosea went to the marketplace of prostitute slaves and bought Gomer off the slave tables. He brought her home, made her his wife, and had children with her. He bought her when she was a disgrace and an embarrassment, and he only asked that she be a good wife to him. Hosea offered Gomer a new life of honor before God and man.

God used Hosea to demonstrate how deep and unconditional His love was for Israel. He desired them even when they had forsaken Him, turned to false gods, and had become prostitutes in their worship. Through Hosea, God was saying to them, "Even though you have disgraced Me and embarrassed Me, I love you and I want you to marry Me. I want to give you a new life of honor."

God has always desired a people who would live in a loving relationship with Him: "Thou art my people; and they shall say, Thou art my God" (Hosea 2:23). And that desire found full expression in Christ Jesus. With His sinless blood He "bought" us out of the marketplace of sin and "spiritual prostitution," our worship of false gods and our pursuit of evil practices. Paul wrote about our Savior to the Ephesians:

> *In whom we have redemption through his blood, the forgiveness of sins, according to the riches of his grace.*
>
> EPHESIANS 1:7

Jesus redeemed us, purchased us, paid the full price for us, and took us out of the sin market and bondage of the devil, the world, and our flesh. He purchased us with His life so that we might be free to love Him and become His bride, the Church. As slaves to sin, we were ruled by the devil, who tormented us, lied to us, stole from us, and tried to destroy us with shame. As the bride of Jesus Christ, we are ruled by His love. Our magnificent Lord imparts His righteous nature through the indwelling of the Holy Spirit, who leads us, counsels us, and comforts us. As His bride, He gives us a place of honor, and we are to bring glory and honor to Him.

WE ARE HIS BETROTHED

As believers in Jesus Christ, we are betrothed to Him, and we are to walk as those who are promised to Him and Him alone. In biblical times, betrothal meant something very different from what it means today. It was not just an engagement, but the formal part of the marriage ritual. From the moment the man and woman were betrothed, the two were considered one. However, the marriage was usually not consummated for a year or more.

During the betrothal period, the groom would build a home for the couple and continue courting his bride, getting to know her and allowing her to know him as much as possible. The bride would purify and prepare herself for her groom, and one of the best examples of this is found in the book of Esther. The king chose her for his queen, but she spent many months preparing herself for him. No doubt she learned all she could about him so that she could please him in all respects. Finally, when the groom brought his bride to their new home and they began to physically live as husband and wife, all controversies had been laid to rest. They began their new life together in peace.

When we understand the meaning of betrothal, we see that our marriage to Jesus will be consummated physically when we receive our glorified bodies at the resurrection. Yet we are married to Him now. In biblical times, if either the bride or groom had sexual relations with someone else during their betrothal, it was considered adultery. So we must view our betrothal to Jesus as a sacred covenant of marriage, sealed by His blood and the Holy Spirit who makes us one. Yet we groan for the time when our marriage will be fully consummated at the resurrection and we partake of the Marriage Supper of the Lamb.

Until then, Jesus is fulfilling His part of our betrothal. Before His ascension, He told us He was going to prepare a place for us, and He is always praying and interceding for us. He is continuing to court us, to woo us, to lavish His love upon us, and to bring us into "the knowledge of Him" as much as possible. All His attentions are toward our purification and preparation for His coming.

And what is our part of the betrothal? Remember the parable of the ten virgins? We are to keep our lamps lit with the fire of the Holy Spirit and renew our minds with God's Word. We are to pray without ceasing, rejoice at all times, and love one another as He loves us. We are to be continuously aware that we are Jesus' bride and a reflection of His nature, truth, and glory on the earth.

DIVINE REFLECTION

> **Be** ye therefore followers of God, as dear children;
> And walk in love, as Christ also hath loved us, and
> hath given himself for us an offering and a sacrifice to
> God for a sweetsmelling savour.
>
> EPHESIANS 5:1-2

Why is it so critical that we follow and imitate Jesus? Because anything we do reflects on Him. We are His betrothed. He gets the glory every time we restrain ourselves from doing and saying what we should not say and do. He receives honor when we humble ourselves and reckon our flesh dead. We present an especially strong witness of His goodness when we love our enemies and those who hate us, persecute us, or reject us. Unfortunately, He also gets a bad reputation when we act badly.

When we walk in the ways of our own fleshly desires and lusts, giving in to selfish ambitions and reactions and behavior, we bring no glory to Jesus, and we certainly do not have His approval or receive His favor. What is worse, we separate ourselves from fellowship with Him. This does not mean He ceases to love us or even loves us less. He loves us with unconditional, merciful, and longsuffering love at all times. Our sinful, unloving actions, however, keep us from the rewards that come from righteous living and loving as He loves.

A single person only has their own reputation to worry about — what they say and do reflects only on themselves. But a married person's behavior and words also reflect on their spouse. No man wants his wife running around town, writing bad checks, engaging in filthy conversation, getting drunk and obnoxious in public, or flirting with or dating other men. He wants his wife to refrain from those behaviors because he loves her and wants her reputation to be good, but he also wants his wife to be a godly reflection of him and their family.

A wife doesn't want her husband flirting with or dating other women, getting in trouble with the law, gambling their family income away, smoking dope, or staying out all night at pool halls. She wants him to enjoy a fine reputation and be a man of the highest integrity for his own sake and for her sake and their children's. Every woman wants to be proud of her husband.

We are eternally blessed that our Bridegroom is perfect. His reputation is stellar in all respects, His character unblemished, His strength and courage unmatched, and His love for us beyond our imagination. Our betrothal to Jesus Christ demands that we no longer live for ourselves, but for Him. We are to separate ourselves from filthiness or foolishness of any type because what we do reflects upon Him.

LEARNING WHAT'S HONORABLE

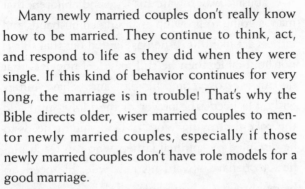

Many newly married couples don't really know how to be married. They continue to think, act, and respond to life as they did when they were single. If this kind of behavior continues for very long, the marriage is in trouble! That's why the Bible directs older, wiser married couples to mentor newly married couples, especially if those newly married couples don't have role models for a good marriage.

If you take two people who come from backgrounds in which daddy was drunk most of the time and was abusive all the time, or in which mama was running the streets and was rarely home...if you take two people who come from broken homes or whose parents had a frigid, formal relationship...if you take two people who come from homes where manipulation took place, drugs were sold, or where pornography and filthy behavior were manifested, those two people have absolutely no understanding of what it means to have a godly marriage or how to treat each other in a way that pleases the Lord. They need to be taught how to be married.

If a man has a father who was never faithful to his mother, was gone from the home much of the time at the race track or the local bar, and who came home only to act in a domineering, manipulative, abusive way toward his wife and children, that man is going to grow up assuming all husbands and fathers act like this. If he has figured out that this is not honorable, then he still may feel hopeless that he can ever overcome his past and behave differently. He needs the power of the Holy Spirit and the yoke-destroying Word of God, and he needs to be discipled by spiritual fathers who can teach him how to behave toward his new wife. He needs to be taught what is honorable.

If a woman has a mother who cheats on her daddy, manipulates daddy for everything she wants from him, and speaks badly about daddy the minute he's out of earshot, that woman is going to grow up assuming all wives act like mama acts. Worse, she may be convicted by the Holy Spirit that these ways are evil, but feel trapped in this generational, cursed behavior. That's when the Word and the Spirit step in, she gets delivered from the curse, and Jesus brings spiritual mamas into her life to teach her how to be an honorable wife.

As Jesus' betrothed, we are no different! When we accept Him as our Lord and Savior, He has purchased us out of the slave market and given us His name, but we need to be taught how to live in an honorable marriage relationship with Him and bring glory and honor to His name. There are those who believe in and love Jesus as their Savior who continue to live impure lives not because they are choosing to sin, but simply because they have never been taught properly to distinguish between what is right and wrong in God's eyes. They still smoke and drink and curse and chew and run with those who do...they still whine, complain, and wallow in self-pity every time circumstances don't go their way because they have not learned that such things are dishonorable to their Lord.

When a person becomes a Christian, their immorality and sin don't just naturally dissipate. Sin has to be "put away." The old man has to be stripped away and godly behavior has to be put on just as a person might take off old, dirty, tattered garments and put on new and spotless clothes. We read about this repeatedly in Paul's writings, especially in Ephesians:

> **P**ut off concerning the former conversation the old man, which is corrupt according to the deceitful lusts;
> And be renewed in the spirit of your mind;
> And that ye put on the new man, which after God is created in righteousness and true holiness.
>
> EPHESIANS 4:22-24

At the time of Jesus' crucifixion, the veil that separated the inner court and the Holy of Holies was rent into two pieces, signifying to all believers that they have direct access to God the Father and may live in intimate relationship with Him. There isn't a moment in our lives when we are not in direct association with the Lord. We are always in His presence — Christ in us and us in Christ. Therefore, our very life is to be a life of holiness and service. Never should we lay aside our garments of a holy life and live according to the world system and our flesh. We are always to be exemplifying the new life of honor we have received through Jesus — at home, at work, at church, and in our communities.

Any person who is married in their heart and not merely in their words and by the law knows that they are married at all times. There isn't a moment in that person's life when they are not aware of the impact their words and actions have upon their spouse and family. In our relationship with Christ Jesus, we are His bride at all times, in all situations, in all places, with our whole being. It is our joy to represent Him well and bring honor to His name.

REVIVAL

Before we go any further, I must address the meaning of revival. Many people perceive revival as a mighty move of the Holy Spirit upon unbelievers which brings in a tremendous harvest of souls. This is partially true. But revival is actually a powerful, life-transforming, purifying move of the Holy Spirit upon believers. Then, when the Church becomes holy, purified, bold, and passionate about Jesus, He empowers them to bring in the harvest of souls and disciple them.

Many believers and many churches today must have revival because they have no concept of what it means to live as the betrothed of Jesus Christ. They know what it means to live a religious life — they get baptized, go to church on Sundays, put something in the offering plate, own a Bible, and even read it and pray from time to time. They know what it means to "play church." They know when to stand up and sit down during the services. They know how to address the clergy and which day communion is served. But they don't understand the new life of honor their Savior and Lord has given them. They don't understand their betrothal to Him, and therefore they do not have His purity and power in their lives.

Married life is different from single life in the natural and in the Lord. A single person can go and do pretty much what they want to do, any time of the day or night. They can spend their money any way they want, without asking anybody's opinion, getting anybody's approval, or consulting with anybody about timing or method or consequences. That's not true for a married person. A married person is no longer alone but part of a union in which husband and wife hold all things in common and do all things in consideration of one another. Furthermore, the married person divorces themselves completely from their old life and bonds with their spouse.

As believers, we must sever all relationship with sin and the world and walk in righteousness, peace, and joy with our Lord. Hosea knew that for the Israelites to come back to God, their husband, they would have to spurn idolatry, the worship of other gods. For Gomer to be fulfilled in her marriage to Hosea, she would have to turn from her form of idolatry, going after other lovers and the money they brought her. Paul wrote to the Ephesians:

> **B**e ye therefore followers of God, as dear children;
> And walk in love, as Christ also hath loved us, and hath given himself for us an offering and a sacrifice to God for a sweetsmelling savour.
> But fornication, and all uncleanness, or covetousness, let it not be once named among you, as becometh saints;
> Neither filthiness, nor foolish talking, nor jesting, which are not convenient: but rather giving of thanks.
> For this ye know, that no whoremonger, nor unclean person, nor covetous man, who is an idolater, hath any inheritance in the kingdom of Christ and of God.
>
> EPHESIANS 5:1-5

We cannot live betrothed to Jesus and continue "dating" this philosophy and flirting with that idol. We must put off the old man and put on the new. We cannot neglect studying the Word of God, and it is essential to the well-being of our relationship with Christ that we are sensitive and obedient to the Holy Spirit. We must engage in intimate prayer and have regular fellowship with other believers. And we must not continue in sin of any kind, whether in our thoughts, our speech, or our deeds.

The honor Jesus bestows upon us as His beloved demands an honorable life in return. Has the Church today lived this new life of honor before the world? Only God can judge the hearts of humanity, but as for me and my house, we are seeking revival! We are hungry for more and more of God, and as our Bridegroom illuminates this sin and that oppression and this lie and that error, we are repenting! We are turning from our idolatry! We are crushing our flesh! We are on our faces praying for wisdom and compassion and mercy and grace to walk in this heavenly and totally undeserved gift, this new life of honor. When Jesus returns, we want our lamps to be lit with bonfires of passion for Him and Him alone!

3

SACRIFICIAL
LOVE

When we get all dressed up to attend a wedding, we put on our very best clothes and behavior because we are going to take part in a sacred act. A man and a woman are going to give their lives to one another for as long as they live, and we have the honor to stand with them and witness their solemn, sacred pledge to each other. They are going to make a covenant, a holy and irrevocable vow, to be one, to own all things in common, and to love and care for one another for the rest of their lives.

Throughout the Scriptures, the shedding of blood was required for a covenant to be in effect. That's why it is called the "cutting" of covenant. The covenant on which our relationship with the Lord is based involves the sacrificial shedding of Jesus' blood on the cross. In a marriage, the covenant was fulfilled when a husband penetrated his virgin wife and she bled. Furthermore, in ancient times, after the husband and wife had consummated their marriage vows, it was the husband's responsibility to wash away the blood from his wife's body and apply healing ointment or oil to her before she appeared in public again. First, washing with water; then, anointing with oil. Does this sound familiar?

The Lord spoke to His people through the prophet Ezekiel about the way He had raised them up to be His bride. As you read through these verses, note that all of the aspects of a covenant marriage are included in this passage of Scripture:

> I have caused thee to multiply as the bud of the field, and thou hast increased and waxen great, and thou art come to excellent ornaments: thy breasts are fashioned, and thine hair is grown, whereas thou wast naked and bare.
>
> Now when I passed by thee, and looked upon thee, behold, thy time was the time of love; and I spread my skirt over thee, and covered thy nakedness: yea, I sware unto thee, and entered into a covenant with thee, saith the Lord God, and thou becamest mine.
>
> Then washed I thee with water; yea, I thoroughly washed away thy blood from thee, and I anointed thee with oil.
>
> I clothed thee also with broidered work, and shod thee with badgers' skin, and I girded thee about with fine linen, and I covered thee with silk.
>
> I decked thee also with ornaments, and I put bracelets upon thy hands, and a chain on thy neck.

And I put a jewel on thy forehead, and earrings in thine ears, and a beautiful crown upon thine head.

Thus wast thou decked with gold and silver; and thy raiment was of fine linen, and silk, and broidered work; thou didst eat fine flour, and honey, and oil: and thou wast exceeding beautiful, and thou didst prosper into a kingdom.

And thy renown went forth among the heathen for thy beauty: for it was perfect through my comeliness, which I had put upon thee, saith the Lord God.

EZEKIEL 16:7-14

In our relationship with Jesus, the union that is made possible for us because of His shed blood is followed by the waters of baptism and the sealing oil of the Holy Spirit on our lives. It is the Lord who dresses us and makes us presentable as His chosen bride, a bride dressed in splendor and glory. We are incredibly and remarkably blessed as a beloved bride who is bestowed great value.

PREPARING FOR OUR BRIDEGROOM

Through the centuries, the Church has been called the bride of Christ, and this term is based largely upon a parable Jesus taught in which He identified Himself — the Son of man — as coming for a bride who is *anticipating* and *preparing* for His coming:

Then shall the kingdom of heaven be likened unto ten virgins, which took their lamps, and went forth to meet the bridegroom.

And five of them were wise, and five were foolish.

They that were foolish took their lamps, and took no oil with them:

But the wise took oil in their vessels with their lamps.

While the bridegroom tarried, they all slumbered and slept.

And at midnight there was a cry made, Behold, the bridegroom cometh; go ye out to meet him.

Then all those virgins arose, and trimmed their lamps.

And the foolish said unto the wise, Give us of your oil; for our lamps are gone out.

But the wise answered, saying, Not so; lest there be not enough for us and you: but go ye rather to them that sell, and buy for yourselves.

And while they went to buy, the bridegroom came; and they that were ready went in with him to the marriage: and the door was shut.

Afterward came also the other virgins, saying, Lord, Lord, open to us.

But he answered and said, Verily I say unto you, I know you not.

Watch therefore, for ye know neither the day nor the hour wherein the Son of man cometh.

MATTHEW 25:1-13

What a glorious truth that we are the bride of Christ! But how are we to prepare to be Jesus' bride? How do we keep our lamps lit brightly with the oil of the Holy Spirit? Paul answers this in his letter to the Ephesians:

> **B**e ye therefore followers of God, as dear children;
> And walk in love, as Christ also hath loved us, and
> hath given himself for us an offering and a sacrifice to
> God for a sweetsmelling savour.
>
> EPHESIANS 5:1-2

Paul tells us to keep our lamps lit with love. We are a part of the greatest love story ever told! As believers betrothed to Jesus we are to think and speak and act with a constant motivation of love and adoration and worship toward Him. But this isn't an emotional head-in-the-clouds or floating-on-air kind of love. Romance in the movies pales in the face of the love of our Savior and Lord! This is *agape* love. The love God has for His children and the love with which Jesus loves us is a sacrificial love.

Agape love is generous, unending, unconditional love. It is loving as Jesus loved us and gave Himself as an offering, a "sweetsmelling" sacrifice to God on our behalf. To love others as Jesus loves us is to love not as we desire, but as He desires us to love. This kind of love does not depend upon receiving love in return. *Agape* love flows from the very heart and character of God because He is love. *Agape* is a commitment to love, a decision to love regardless of the circumstances.

"It's simple," Paul says. "Just follow Jesus. If you don't know how to be a Christian, just imitate Him. Treat other people the way He has treated you, the way He has loved and forgiven you." Paul wrote to the Corinthians:

> **B**lessed be God, even the Father of our Lord Jesus Christ, the Father of mercies, and the God of all comfort;
>
> Who comforteth us in all our tribulation, that we may be able to comfort them which are in any trouble, by the comfort wherewith we ourselves are comforted of God.

2 CORINTHIANS 1:3-4

The Holy Spirit may prompt us to express our love toward another person even when we are going through a trial. Yet we make ourselves available to comfort others at all times with the comfort we are receiving from God. We are sensitive to the Holy Spirit's leading to minister to others in their physical and emotional pain. Then we also are a "sweet-smelling savour" to God, and He will continue to comfort us as we comfort others.

As we love others and love God, it is important for us to remember that nobody becomes a "sweet-smelling savour" in the nostrils of God without sacrifice, without paying the price. Loving others isn't a great challenge if we can love the people we choose to love, and then love them on our own terms, at the convenient time, place, occasion, and in comfortable conditions. Loving all other believers, those who may be very different from us in culture, race, background, likes, dislikes, and personality differences — and loving them in spite of their faults, sins, and failures — is a tremendous challenge. The challenge is to display the same kind of sacrificial and unconditional love that Jesus lavishes upon us.

We have a tendency to think that some people are just "naturals" when it comes to loving God or loving other people. We think they are just nice people and we wish we could be like them. Those who follow this line of thinking usually use this as an excuse for not being loving. They feel absolved of any responsibility to change. "That's just the way I am. I just don't happen to be that nice. Loving God and others just isn't natural for me. God made me that way and so it's all right that I'm not as loving as some people seem to be." But the Bible is very clear and specific when it comes to the way we love God and love others. Jesus said,

> **A** *new commandment I give unto you, That ye love one another; as I have loved you, that ye also love one another.*
>
> JOHN 13:34

Love is a commandment.

Like all of God's principles and laws, we cannot accomplish the love walk without His supernatural ability. Thank God for the Holy Ghost! The Bible tells us that one of the divine purposes of the Holy Spirit is to manifest the love of God in our hearts so that we can manifest that love toward others. In the book of Romans, Paul tells us how this works:

> **T**herefore being justified by faith, we have peace with God through our Lord Jesus Christ:
>
> By whom also we have access by faith into this grace wherein we stand, and rejoice in hope of the glory of God.
>
> And not only so, but we glory in tribulations also; knowing that tribulation worketh patience;
>
> And patience, experience; and experience, hope:
>
> And hope maketh not ashamed; because the love of God is shed abroad in our hearts by the Holy Ghost which is given unto us.
>
> ROMANS 5:1-5

God has given us an unlimited, divine capacity to love, but we must make the effort to develop that love, to release that love, and to walk in that love at all times. To love is a choice we make with our will. So many people seem to be waiting on something to happen in their lives so they will automatically feel more love for others, and then out of that feeling, they assume they will show love more spontaneously and generously. That isn't the way it works! The love of Jesus Christ is not going to suddenly envelop us to the point where we become floating angelic-like beings who walk through life with wonderful smiles on our faces and wonderful attitudes in our hearts.

The truth of the matter is that often the greatest sacrifice we make is choosing to love. Love requires each of us to nail our will to the cross and obey God's commandment to love — regardless of the nature of the people we encounter, regardless of how we feel in any given moment, and regardless of the circumstances and situations surrounding us. But when we decide to live the *agape* lifestyle and put away the old "me-first" lifestyle, the full joy and power of God's love will come pouring through our lives. God's released love will not only transform our lives, but the lives of those we touch — and we will be a bride whose lamp is lit with His glory!

THE LANGUAGE OF LOVE

When you observe an engaged couple, you are going to see some things that will tickle you and touch your heart at the same time. They have a way of speaking to one another and showing affection to one another; and there is a certain sparkle in their eyes when they look at one another. This is their language of love.

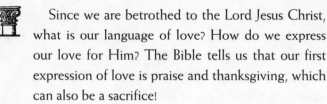

Since we are betrothed to the Lord Jesus Christ, what is our language of love? How do we express our love for Him? The Bible tells us that our first expression of love is praise and thanksgiving, which can also be a sacrifice!

Thus saith the Lord; Again there shall be heard in this place...The voice of joy, and the voice of gladness, the voice of the bridegroom, and the voice of the bride, the voice of them that shall say, Praise the Lord of hosts: for the Lord is good; for his mercy endureth for ever; and of them that shall bring the sacrifice of praise into the house of the Lord.

JEREMIAH 33:10-11, EMPHASIS MINE

By him therefore let us offer the sacrifice of praise to God continually, that is, the fruit of our lips giving thanks to his name.

HEBREWS 13:15

Every spouse needs to hear how they are loved, appreciated, and regarded highly, and Jesus is no exception. He desires to hear from our lips that He is worthy to be praised, deserving of our worship, and valued above all! We express our love in words and in making melody in our hearts. We are to give voice to our love.

How many wives say, "He never tells me he loves me anymore." And if you ask the husband, he'll probably say, "Of course I love her. Why doesn't she know that? I come home every night, I fix what's broken around the house, I make sure there's food on the table." The fact is, we need to hear words of love from our spouse — and it goes both ways. There are countless husbands today who need to hear words of love, encouragement, and appreciation from their wives. They ache to hear that what they do is valued and that who they are is adored.

When we voice our praise and worship to God, we actually open up the gates of our own souls to receive His love for us. The love relationship we have with Him grows and flourishes as we raise our voices in praise and thanksgiving to our Creator, who loved us even when we were sinners and redeemed us from hell and the curses of death and destruction. He seated us with Himself in the heavenlies and took our shame, loneliness, and fear away forever. He filled us with His peace and wrapped us in His glory. Now that is something to shout about!

A second way we offer a sacrifice of love to God is by loving what our Groom loves and hating what He hates. Jesus loves what is righteous, true, and good, and hates what is evil, false, and eternally unproductive. We display our loyalty to our Savior and Lord, who bought us back from slavery and bondage by His precious, sinless blood, when we submit to His will, His ways, and His wisdom completely.

Jesus loves only what is "goodness and righteousness and truth" (Ephesians 5:9). He loves the sinner, even as He hates the sin. He stands against and has no fellowship with the unfruitful works of darkness. And what does He love? People! He loves all who are in relationship with Him and all who are not. What Jesus loves, we are to love. We have to get beyond our prejudices, our personality differences, and our petty offenses and embrace what Jesus embraces. To do so is an act of worship. It is an act of love not only for the person we are serving and encouraging and edifying, but it is an act of love and honor toward our Bridegroom.

Along these same lines, a third way we offer a sacrifice of love to our Bridegroom is by obeying Him, not only obeying the Ten Commandments and all of the statutes written in the Bible, but by obeying what the Holy Spirit speaks to our hearts. We are to do what He tells us to do moment by moment, hour by hour, day by day, week by week, month by month, and year by year. When the Holy Spirit says, "Speak this word to that person," "Go lay hands on that person in Jesus' name," "Go to the hospital and visit that person," or "Call up that person and encourage them," we must obey. Jesus said,

If ye love me, keep my commandments.

He that hath my commandments, and keepeth them, he it is that loveth me: and he that loveth me shall be loved of my Father, and I will love him, and will manifest myself to him.

JOHN 14:15,21

Obedience to the Word and the Spirit is an act of sacrificial love which always bears the fruit of the Spirit. Our acts of sacrificial love toward God's people or unbelievers and our obedience to the Holy Spirit's commands and the Word of God manifest the divine nature of Jesus, our Bridegroom, to the world we touch. When anyone comes in contact with us, they come in contact with the *agape* love of Jesus.

God's character of love works within us to produce the fruit of the Holy Spirit, the divine language of love. The fruit is God's expressed love, the aftereffect and end result of the working of the Holy Spirit in us. Some Christians see the Holy Spirit as the fruit, but the fruit is *of the Spirit*. In the same way my children are my fruit and they express the essence of my life, the fruit of the Spirit is the essence of the Spirit expressed through us. But you wouldn't say that my children are me, and you wouldn't say the fruit of the Spirit *is* the Spirit. Remember, the love of God is shed abroad in our hearts *by* the Holy Spirit.

Furthermore, the fruit is singular because the essence and nature of the Holy Spirit cannot be divided. However, the fruit is expressed in a multi-faceted form, like a diamond of pure agape love with facets, which Paul describes as "love, joy, peace, longsuffering, gentleness, goodness, faith, meekness, and temperance" (Galatians 5:22-23). The fruit of the Spirit is one jewel, brightly shining, which catches the light of the Son and refracts His love, beauty, power, and glory.

The Holy Spirit also desires that we reflect all of His nature simultaneously and without classification. The Christian life is not an exercise in being loving at one hour, joyful the next, at peace the next, showing occasional times of patience and self-control, at other times displaying goodness and faith, and at other times being gentle or meek. No! The Holy Spirit desires to refract our Bridegroom's total, unending, and unchanging nature through us at all times. Our love for God is fruitful. It is not a static abstract thing inside us. It has manifestation. It has productivity. It has expression!

SEPARATION FROM EVIL

Walking in sacrificial, *agape* love and allowing the fruit of the Spirit to grow and develop in our lives has a flip side to it. We are also admonished by Paul to have nothing whatsoever to do with darkness or with anything that is unproductive in God's kingdom.

(For the fruit of the Spirit is in all goodness and righteousness and truth;)
Proving what is acceptable unto the Lord.
And have no fellowship with the unfruitful works of darkness, but rather reprove them.

EPHESIANS 5:9-11

When we are born again and become Jesus' beloved, the enemy has no right to reproduce his fruit in our lives anymore. Anytime we give place to the devil in our lives, we will see the unfruitful works of darkness. And those works are temporal, unsatisfying, unrewarding, and highly limited. There is no eternal value, no lasting fulfillment, and no heavenly reward associated with any work of darkness. In verse 11, the Holy Spirit commands us to "reprove" them.

The fact that the Holy Spirit used the word "reprove" says a lot. It is the Greek word *elengchete,* and this word gives the body of Christ clear and definite marching orders when it comes to the unfruitful works of darkness. *Elengchete* means to expose, to rebuke, to discipline, to convict, to correct, and to expel. There is no compromise with the unfruitful works of darkness! We are to shine the light of God's Word on them and purge them from our lives. Paul goes on to say:

> **F**or it is a shame even to speak of those things which are done of them in secret.
> But all things that are reproved are made manifest by the light: for whatsoever doth make manifest is light.
>
> EPHESIANS 5:12-13

Paul says we are not even to talk about the works of darkness because the light will expose them. In other words, we expose and rebuke by simply speaking the Word and releasing the power of the Holy Spirit into that situation. If the Holy Spirit leads us to actually confront the one who is walking in darkness, we simply tell them what God's Word says and pray for them. And we must always remember that the Word tells us to reprove the works of darkness, not the one who is blinded and lost in the darkness. Our responsibility is to shine God's heavenly flashlight into their darkness so that they can see!

No wife who truly loves her husband is going to be loving and joyful and edifying in her husband's presence and then turn around and gossip about him and downgrade him to her friends. And yet, there are those in the Church who display the fruit of the Spirit when they are in the presence of other believers — oh, they can be syrupy sweet in their words of love and they can wear longsuffering like a badge — but get them in secret with a few of their close friends, and just listen to how the gossip flows!

There are also those who praise the Lord and worship Him with loud voices inside the church house, but get them in their own house and just listen to them: "I don't know why the Lord doesn't meet this need of mine" or "I don't know why God has me working with those crazy, mixed-up people" or "Why does she always have to sing the same song over and over and over?"

To love sacrificially is to love whether we are in public or private. It is to be resolute in mind and heart that God is worthy of praise and thanksgiving whether anybody is listening or not. It is to love and serve God's people whether we are in their presence or not. It is to obey God's commands and to manifest His nature — to bear the fruit of the Holy Spirit — not only in what we say and do, but in the very way we *think* and *believe*. The fruit of the Holy Spirit is to infiltrate and to manifest itself in our *attitudes*.

Are you aware that anything you speak, you intensify — not only outwardly but inwardly. This is one of the key principles at work in the corruption of this present generation. People in our generation are not doing things that people in previous generations didn't do. Those in previous generations sinned in every way people sin today, but they didn't do it on television, they didn't talk about it on talk shows or over dinner, they didn't glamorize their sin, and they didn't write magazine articles about sin, report about sin, or broadcast sin.

In displaying and speaking about sin so freely and so frequently, we intensify it, grow in the knowledge of it, and even become comfortable with it. When we put sin on center stage and talk about it repeatedly, it reproduces because we are having fellowship with the unfruitful works of darkness. We give sin permission to continue and to grow. When we become comfortable with sin, we eventually downplay its consequences as well. We say, "Everybody does it, so it must be all right." The shock value of sin dissipates. We accept sin as normal, routine, and inevitable. None of which are true before God!

Sin is not normal behavior for the believer.

Sin is never to be routine for the believer.

Sin is not inevitable for the believer.

We have been freed from the bonds of sin!

What we believe is always directly influenced by what we hear. Most believers are very familiar with Romans 10:17, "So then faith cometh by hearing." What we hear influences what we believe. The rest of Romans 10:17 is the key for us, "So then faith cometh by hearing, and hearing by the word of God." What we hear influences and establishes what we believe, what we say, and what we do. So our hearing needs to be focused on the Word of God. All other messages about sin need to be tuned out, turned down, and taken out of our lives.

WAKE UP!

What you hear impacts what you believe, and what you believe always impacts what you say and do. We either build ourselves up or tear ourselves down in our spiritual marriage to the Lord and our lives in the body of Christ — depending on what we focus upon. So Paul gives us a wake-up call:

> **W**herefore he saith, Awake thou that sleepest, and arise from the dead, and Christ shall give thee light.
>
> See then that ye walk circumspectly, not as fools, but as wise,
>
> Redeeming the time, because the days are evil.
>
> Wherefore be ye not unwise, but understanding what the will of the Lord is.

EPHESIANS 5:14-17

When you are asleep among dead people, you look like a dead person. Paul is saying, "If you act like the world, you are like a spiritually alive person who is asleep among spiritually dead people. So wake up! Shake off your worldly thinking, attitudes, and behavior and stop acting the fool! Walk in the light of Christ and be wise. Then you'll know what you're supposed to do with your life — and you'll be ready when your Bridegroom comes for you!"

Jesus' heart swells with joy and pride when we think like He thinks, feel what He feels, laugh when He laughs, and act as He acts. It gives Him pleasure when we are a living sacrifice for Him, praising and giving thanks for His grace and mercy, obeying His Word and the Holy Spirit's guiding hand, loving and serving others, separating ourselves from all unfruitful works of darkness, and walking in holiness and purity. And the Bible says when we do this, we will be wise, understanding what the will of God is for our lives and in the situations He places us. Walking in the sacrificial love of Jesus Christ is walking hand in hand with our Bridegroom in the light of His glory — fully awake, fully aware, and full of peace.

4

SUBMISSION

As the bride and body of Christ, we must learn how to relate to our Bridegroom and to each other, and God has chosen submission as the principle of the kingdom which sets the tone for all relationships: God and man, husband and wife, parent and child, employer and employee, pastor and congregation, friend and friend. Jesus taught the importance of submission even in the friend to friend relationship:

> **G**reater love hath no man than this, that a man lay down his life for his friends.
> Ye are my friends, if ye do whatsoever I command you.
>
> JOHN 15:13-14

Jesus sealed His friendship and became worthy to be our Bridegroom by submitting to the will of His Father and shedding His blood for us, the supreme act of love. When we submit to His Word and the leading of the Holy Spirit, He calls us His friend — and He is not talking about some casual acquaintance we play ball with after school! When Jesus used the word "friend," He was talking covenant. Everything that is His is ours and everything that is ours is His. His greatest delight is blessing us, and our greatest joy is pleasing Him and knowing Him. Furthermore, He commands us to love one another as He loves us:

> **A** *new commandment I give unto you, That ye love one another; as I have loved you, that ye also love one another.*
>
> *By this shall all men know that ye are my disciples, if ye have love one to another.*
>
> JOHN 13:34-35

God has established that the Church must operate in the principle of submission — love in action — for the world to see Jesus in us. However, there are some fundamental truths associated with submission that must be established in our hearts and minds for us to walk this powerful walk. Some of these truths seem hard when viewed on the surface, but when we plumb the depths of them, the truth sets us free.

SUBMISSION MEANS WAR!

In speaking to the Ephesians about submission, Paul begins with the body of Christ at large:

And be not drunk with wine, wherein is excess; but be filled with the Spirit;

Speaking to yourselves in psalms and hymns and spiritual songs, singing and making melody in your heart to the Lord;

Giving thanks always for all things unto God and the Father in the name of our Lord Jesus Christ;

Submitting yourselves one to another in the fear of God.

EPHESIANS 5:18-21

Notice that Paul introduces the concept of submission in the context of being filled with the Holy Spirit, making melody in our hearts to the Lord, and giving thanks always. This is a big hint: *We cannot possibly submit to one another in our flesh or our own strength!* We must be hooked up to the supernatural love and ability of Christ Jesus to obey this word from God. Also notice that we submit "in the fear of God." Submission now becomes a sacred, holy act of love and reverence unto our Lord. This is not something we can brush aside and take lightly.

The Greek word for "submitting" gives us even more revelation on the concept. This is the compound word *hupotasso*. In classical Greek, *tasso* is a term which has a military connotation and indicates soldiers or troops being drawn together in order, none breaking rank, turning on each other, or walking in disobedience to those in authority over them. *Hupo* simply means under, which is to subject oneself. So the New Testament meaning is that we are to be subject to one another in the divine callings and order in which our supreme commander, the Lord Jesus Christ, has placed us. We are not to assert ourselves or have a self-centered, independent spirit; but we are to accept His commission to serve humbly and in love toward one another. The picture that comes to mind is the mighty invincible army described in the book of Joel:

> **T**hey shall run like mighty men; they shall climb the wall like men of war; and they shall march every one on his ways, and they shall not break their ranks:
>
> Neither shall one thrust another; they shall walk every one in his path: and when they fall upon the sword, they shall not be wounded.
>
> JOEL 2:7-8

By using the word *hupotasso*, Paul clearly puts this entire passage of Scripture in the context of war. The body of Christ is in a life-and-death struggle against the powers of darkness which rule this world system. And I have noticed something about people when they are thrown together in a war. All of a sudden it doesn't matter what sex you are, what race you are, what color you are, or how smart you are. We're fighting together against an evil that will destroy us all, and my survival and your survival depend on our working together, submitting to one another in the fear of the Lord. Whether God has placed me as your commanding officer or you as mine, we are united by the cause of freedom and subject to one another through the blood of Jesus.

Hupotasso tells us that although God loves us equally and is no respecter of persons, He has subjected us to one another positionally. There are generals and there are foot soldiers. There are sergeants and there are medics. There are captains and there are cooks. We are all equally important and come behind in no spiritual gift — God will have intimate fellowship with us and shower blessings on all of us — but we are subject to one another as He has placed us in the body. We submit to one another in the fear of the Lord, because the Lord has placed us in our callings and has given us our giftings. Paul describes it as a walk of love where every joint supplies what the body needs:

> **B**ut speaking the truth in love, may grow up into him in all things, which is the head, even Christ:
>
> From whom the whole body fitly joined together and compacted by that which every joint supplieth, according to the effectual working in the measure of every part, maketh increase of the body unto the edifying of itself in love.

 EPHESIANS 4:15-16

In peacetime, we can all sit around, love and worship the Lord, and our equality in Christ is very obvious. It's easy to love one another because His love and grace and blessings are evident in all of our lives. We are all content and fulfilled. However, when we are at war, God establishes rank and file and the tempter comes to say, "You see, you are not being treated as an *equal* because you have to submit to a person who is not as smart, not as hard-working, or not as spiritual as you are. God made you *equal* to this other person, so you should not have to submit to them." The enemy knows that if he can confuse the issues of equality and submission, he can cause us to turn on one another, rebel against authority, and cause our defeat.

Peacetime does not require submission. War requires submission. There is no submission when there is no disagreement or conflict. Don't tell me you are submitting when everything is going your way, on your timetable, according to your plan! That is not submission. That is agreement. That is a path with no resistance from anything or anybody. No, submission can only occur when there is disagreement, and disagreement comes as a result of the fallen nature of man. As long as we are living in these death-doomed bodies which contain the nature of the flesh and work contrary to God's kingdom, we are in a state of war. We must discipline our flesh to submit to our spirit and to the will of God. We must discipline our flesh to submit to each other in the knowledge that we are Jesus' beloved.

Like it or not, God has placed us in situations where we must submit to win the war. We must reverse the five rebellious "I wills" of Lucifer (see Isaiah 14:13-14), which seek to rule from the old nature of our flesh, and come into line with Jesus', "Not My will, but Thy will be done, Father." (See Luke 22:42.) We must understand that when we submit to this person or that person, we are submitting to the Lord. We are operating in the fear of the Lord. We are trusting Him and placing our lives in His hands — the only safe place in the universe.

HOW A WIFE SUBMITS

After introducing the concept of submission in terms of winning the war, Paul then begins to elaborate on three specific areas where the believer must understand and walk in submission: husbands and wives, parents and children, and masters and servants. He tackles husbands and wives first, which is perhaps the most controversial of the three today and the subject of our discussion.

> **W**ives, submit yourselves unto your own husbands, as unto the Lord.
>
> For the husband is the head of the wife, even as Christ is the head of the church: and he is the saviour of the body.
>
> Therefore as the church is subject unto Christ, so let the wives be to their own husbands in every thing.
>
> EPHESIANS 5:22-24

In writing about submission, Paul is not talking about dominance of gender, but about corporate relationship and structure within a family. To submit is to make ourselves vulnerable to the needs and desires of others. It is to yield in the decision-making, problem-solving, directional aspects of a relationship. A husband and wife are in a government relationship — both cannot exert the same degree of authority simultaneously.

By the necessity born of two people being in one relationship, one person must submit to the governance of the other in facing problems, decisions, and conflicts. The natural minds of people in this generation want to put husband and wife on the same playing field, both playing umpire at the same time. Can you imagine a baseball game with two umpires standing behind the plate? Husband and wife do not play the same position when it comes to making decisions, manifesting authority, or taking responsibility.

Many women believe that to submit to their husbands is to lie down, roll over, and play dead. By submitting to her husband's decision, she has acknowledged, accepted, and approved his domination of her and sealed her inferiority to him. She has allowed her identity to be dwarfed or destroyed by his ego and selfishness. This is the lie the devil would like all wives to swallow because it naturally incites resentment and rebellion.

But understood correctly, submission is a freedom word, a deliverance word, a word of position and function that brings a woman to higher and higher levels of intimacy with the Lord and greater power and influence in her marriage. Submission is about compliance, cooperation, and exceeding influence. And when the kingdom principle of submission is followed, harmony and unity in spirit can be reached even when there is disagreement. Moreover, there are times when a husband and wife, parent and child, or employer and employee can eventually come into full agreement because they are walking in submission.

So much of the time we don't see the whole picture; our spouse has part of it and we have part of it. In the beginning we each may see the situation differently, but as we pray and talk together, sharing what the Lord is showing us, seeking the mind of Christ and the truth, we can see the whole picture and come into agreement. Open discussion, prayer, and progressive revelation often will bring any relationship into harmony and unity.

But what happens if there is prayer, discussion, revelation, and still no agreement? What if the husband is an unbeliever and won't even pray? What if the husband is saved and loves God, but spends all his free time in front of the television set or at the ball games, neglecting the things of God and refusing to grow up? What if he asks her to do something immoral or illegal?

To me, it is obvious that no believer should ever submit to a request or a behavior that is ungodly, evil, or unholy. If the husband demands that his wife drink or do drugs with him, if he wants her to have sex with someone else, or if he tells her to assist him in committing a crime or telling a lie, she must respectfully say no. The Bible never commands a believer to submit to evil, immoral commands. The apostle Peter does not say, "Rob banks with your husband so he'll see the love of God in you"! No, he says that it is a wife's "chaste conversation," or pure, innocent, modest, and clean behavior which influences her husband to do right and come to God:

Likewise, ye wives, be in subjection to your own husbands; that, if any obey not the word, they also may without the word be won by the conversation of the wives;

While they behold your chaste conversation coupled with fear.

1 PETER 3:1-2

The most powerful people in the world are wives who know how to submit to the Lord and their husbands! How many men have been won to the Lord through their wives, who treated them like kings and yet refused to do anything that would compromise the Word of God? How many men have seen tremendous success in their business and ministry because they had a praying, godly wife standing with them, giving them wise counsel?

Now what if the husband is a big, burly carpenter who comes home drunk and takes punches at his wife because he's mad at the world? What if he's a deacon in the church, knows all the religious talk and walk, but when he's home he throws his wife across the room when she aggravates him? No wife should submit to this treatment! If that is going on in your home, go see your pastor and get some counsel immediately — with or without your husband. Jesus does not beat His bride!

...and the wife see that she reverence her husband.

EPHESIANS 5:33

This word "reverence" means to respect. This is an attitude, not an action. You can honor your husband's position as your husband and move out of the house to avoid being beaten. You can have a submissive attitude toward your husband and refuse to obey him in an evil act. "Honey, I love you, but I will not do this thing which is illegal and immoral." Do you see how the husband is impacted by God's love and truth all at the same time? Again, you must never underestimate the powerful influence of a submissive, loving wife who knows how to reverence her husband.

WHAT ARE WE SHOWING THE WORLD?

Now why is this so important in the context of our marriage to the Lord Jesus Christ? A wife represents a typology of what the Church is to Jesus. If she rises up and attempts to dominate her husband, she is painting a picture of rebellion against her eternal husband, Jesus, before the world. To rebel is to say, "My way is as good as or better than God's way. I have the right to choose my own destiny and to walk according to my own laws and statutes. I am the lord of my own life and nobody rules over me. I can know as much as God and have as much power as God." None of these statements are truth —

they are lies that flow from the original lie Satan posed in the Garden of Eden: You will be as gods. (See Genesis 3:5.)

There is never any justification for a believer in Christ Jesus to show anything but the utmost respect for Him. After all, He is the *perfect* Husband. His Word is truth; all His ways are perfect; and He is love personified. There is absolutely no reason why a believer should not only submit but also obey the Lord at all times. Believers seem to be almost too casual in their response to the Lord sometimes. He is our Bridegroom and Friend, but He is also our Lord. We are always in a position of submission to Him. We must never assume He exists to serve us or to do our bidding. We exist to serve Him. All things are from Him, and all things are for Him.

The wife's submission is "as unto the Lord." Throughout Paul's writings we find the phrases "as unto" or "like as" or "according to." These phrases are ones he uses to link the practical manifestations of godly behavior to the deeper mysteries of our relationship with the Lord. Everything we do to others is as unto the Lord. There should be a holy fear of God that comes on a wife who entertains the idea of rebelling against her husband when his request does not violate God's Word. And when the request does violate God's Word, there should still be a holy fear of God in her that says, "You do not have to obey, but you still must reverence him." Wives who understand this and practice submission know the awesome reward it brings. God always honors and blesses the wife who submits with incredible favor and influence.

ONE LORD AT ALL TIMES

Wives, submit yourselves to your own husbands, as unto the Lord.

EPHESIANS 5:22

Another vital issue Paul raises in his writings on marriage is that the wife is to be submitted to her husband — not to all men. All women are not to be submitted to all men, but each wife to her own husband. Why? Because they are one. They are fused together, they fit together, they are in a bonded relationship that has an order and structure to it. "Husband and wife" is not the same as "man and woman," nor is it the same as "all men and all women." Paul does not say that a woman is to submit to a man, or all women are to submit to all men. He says that a *wife* should submit to her *husband*.

Submission for the believer is always a covenant relationship, and a wife is called to submit to her husband, the only man with whom she has a marriage covenant relationship. It is the marriage covenant that gives a wife the security she needs to submit. In the same manner, again, believers in Christ Jesus are to be submitted to Christ alone — not to other lords, but to our Lord — because we are His beloved. We are one with Him, we are in a bonded, covenant relationship with Him that has order and structure to it.

Therefore as the church is subject unto Christ, so let the wives be to their own husbands in every thing.

EPHESIANS 5:24

Again we see how a wife being subject to her husband gives the world a picture of how the Church is subject to Jesus Christ. Then Paul goes on to say that the wife is subject to her husband "in every thing." As we are subject to Christ Jesus in everything, so is the wife subject to her husband in all things. There is no room for rebellion! We cannot "fudge" on the "small things." And there is no room for a rebellious attitude any more than there is room for rebellious words or actions.

When a wife submits to her husband in all things, she is saying to the world, "The Church submits to the Lord Jesus Christ in all things. There isn't any facet of the Church that is run according to human wisdom, ability, decision-making, or reasoning. All is submitted to Jesus Christ so that His will might be done in all, through all, and for all who are part of His body."

The strongest witness a Christian wife can give to an unbelieving (or rebellious Christian) husband — and to the unbelievers she touches every day — is her character, speaking in love and living a modest life, with a submissive and quiet spirit. A godly wife's submission becomes a testimony to her husband and extends far beyond their home to the world at large. Their family, friends, neighbors, and colleagues at work see that her husband lives with a godly woman, a fine Christian woman, a loving and helpful and exemplary wife.

Likewise, ye wives, be in subjection to your own husbands; that, if any obey not the word, they also may without the word be won by the conversation of the wives;

While they behold your chaste conversation coupled with fear,

Whose adorning let it not be that outward adorning of plaiting the hair, and of wearing of gold, or of putting on of apparel;

But let it be the hidden man of the heart, in that which is not corruptible, even the ornament of a meek and quiet spirit, which is in the sight of God of great price.

For after this manner in the old time the holy women also, who trusted in God, adorned themselves, being in subjection unto their own husbands:

*Even as Sara obeyed Abraham, calling him lord:
whose daughters ye are, as long as ye do well, and are
not afraid with any amazement.*

1 PETER 3:1-6

Christian wives are to emulate Sara, who obeyed Abraham and called him lord with no fear. When a wife fully trusts the Lord and His plan for her life, submitting to her husband as unto the Lord, she can submit to her husband with great faith. And when a wife submits to her husband in faith, God can move mountains in that husband's life! On the other hand, if she doesn't follow this plan, she brings discredit to the Lord and her testimony becomes tarnished before the very ones she desires most to accept the Lord. More than that, because she is walking in fear and rebellion instead of faith and obedience, she has tied God's hands and He cannot move in her husband's life.

Most rebellion among believers in Christ Jesus isn't what we might recognize as "major rebellion." Most of our rebellion is in the way we think and the way we feel and the way we respond in the "little things" of life. Likewise, most rebellion we see in Christian wives is not always recognized as rebellion.

"I don't care what my husband thinks about the style of my hair or the way that I dress. I'm going to do my own thing."

"I don't care if my husband doesn't like green beans. I'm going to cook them anyway and he'll just have to eat them."

"I don't need to ask my husband about making that commitment of his time or money."

When a wife rebels against a husband's wishes, desires, and his position as a decision-maker, she undermines his authority over the family and diminishes his responsibility. Godly authority is always balanced by responsibility. What we have authority over, we are responsible for, and the man who is made to feel or believe that he has no authority over his family is a man who takes far less responsibility for his family.

Many wives seem to want it both ways. They want their husbands to assume great responsibility for what goes on in the family, but they don't want their husband to have any authority over them or over the family as a whole. A godly marriage doesn't work that way! Believers sometimes fall into this same trap. They want God to do all kinds of things for them — blessings and miracles and acts of deliverance of all sorts. They want God to manifest His responsibility for them, but they have absolutely no desire to submit to His authority by doing what He desires them to do and walking in the ways He directs them to walk.

When we submit to Jesus in all things, we will see Him move heaven and earth to bless us in every aspect of our lives. And the same principle applies to a husband and a wife. When the wife submits to her husband and lets everyone know he is the head of the family, that husband will stand up, take responsibility, bless her and their family — and the world will see it and take note that Jesus is there.

SUBMISSION IS LOVE

Ultimately every person is required to submit. The husband isn't free of all responsibility to submit, but is commanded to submit to the elders of the church if he is saved, to his boss, or to his board of directors if he's the boss. In addition, every husband is required to submit himself directly to the Lord. Remember, saved or not saved, one day that husband of yours will stand face to face with Jesus Christ to give account of his life!

When we examine the dynamics of submission, we see that it is a choice, just like love is a choice. Because life is not always a bowl of cherries and coming up roses, marriage is not always heavenly bliss! We must choose to love our spouse in the good times and the bad. In the same manner, a godly wife chooses to submit to her husband because she chooses to love him as she loves Jesus.

Her husband is her bridegroom on earth; Jesus is her eternal Bridegroom. If she submits to one, she submits to the other, and the love of God is manifest to the world.

In one of Peter's discourses on godly marriages, he concludes with this same overriding theme:

> *Finally, be ye all of one mind, having compassion one of another, love as brethren, be pitiful, be courteous:*
>
> *Not rendering evil for evil, or railing for railing: but contrariwise blessing: knowing that ye are thereunto called, that ye should inherit a blessing.*
>
> 1 PETER 3:8-9

To be "pitiful" is to be tenderhearted. Our love for one another naturally causes us to submit to one another. Submission is a derivative of love. It is part of love and it flows from love.

> *Love is patient, love is kind. It does not envy, it does not boast, it is not proud.*
>
> *It is not rude, it is not self-seeking, it is not easily angered, it keeps no record of wrongs.*
>
> *Love does not delight in evil but rejoices with the truth.*
>
> *It always protects, always trusts, always hopes, always perseveres.*
>
> *Love never fails.*
>
> 1 CORINTHIANS 13:4-8 NIV

Love is willing to yield. It is not selfish, demanding, or self-centered. Lust, on the other hand, is always based upon self-need and self-gratification.

What self wants, self acts to get. Love, in contrast, seeketh not her own. It is willing to submit. Love is always more concerned about the care and welfare of the other person in a relationship. And when a wife submits to her husband, she expresses her love and reverence for him and for the Lord Jesus Christ.

5

GIVING YOUR LIFE

After discussing the powerful principle of submission, I hope you wives do not feel like you've been through the spin cycle in a washing machine! Submission is not easy because we human beings do not like to crucify our flesh. But in case you feel you have the hardest part of the bargain by having to submit to your husband, and in case you are a husband thinking, "Yeah, right, she needs to submit to me right now!" let's dive into the husband's role in all of this.

How often, husband, do you crucify your desires, your plans, and your way of doing things in order to love your wife? Do you *tell* her what *your* plans are for the weekend, or do you *ask* her what *she* had in mind? When you come home from work, do you turn the television on and turn yourself off? Is the only reason you touch her to have sex with her? And here's the big one: When was the last time you just sat with her and really *listened* to her?

Paul writes more verses about husbands than wives in his letter to the Ephesians, and I believe there is a good reason for this. Husbands, the question we must all ask ourselves is this: What am I giving my wife to submit *to?* Our Lord Jesus Christ has pursued us, showed us how to walk in the Spirit and according to God's will and Word, laid His life down for us, paid our debt of sin, risen from the dead to give us new life, and then raised us and seated us in the heavenlies. He has made us joint-heirs — and that's something to submit to!

Now, as husbands, we come to the stark realization that to play the part of Jesus Christ in a marriage is a superhuman feat, something we cannot possibly accomplish without God's guidance and empowerment. This is a monumental assignment from heaven! So let's just take one verse at a time in Ephesians and let the apostle Paul break this down for us.

SELFLESSNESS

Husbands, love your wives, even as Christ also loved the church, and gave himself for it.

EPHESIANS 5:25

The specific language Paul has chosen in the Greek indicates that husbands are to love their wives *continually*. This is an ongoing process of showing her care and comfort and proclaiming his devotion to her. But is it ever possible for a husband to give his life for his wife as Jesus gave Himself for the Church? On the one hand, we would have to say no because no man can give his life to save his wife from her sins. Husbands have died so their wives might live, but no man has the capacity to be the savior of his wife or of any other person. Jesus Christ alone is Savior. On the other hand, we would have to say that it is possible for a man to crucify his flesh and *die to self* for the sake of his wife.

Self is difficult to control, and it is even more difficult to sacrifice! We each want what we want, and this seems to be especially true for us men. We don't like having to give up our precious, valuable, very important lives for the sake of anyone. I'm not talking about begrudgingly giving up a little time when our wives ask for a little time, or resenting it when we decide to set aside our personal agendas to accommodate the desire of our wives. Paul describes marriage as total sacrifice of self for love of a wife — willingly. And there's only one way we can do this. We must trust God. Just as Jesus trusted God — for the joy that was set before Him He endured the cross — we must trust God that by giving our lives away we will gain them. Jesus said,

Whoever clings to his life shall lose it, and whoever loses his life shall save it.

LUKE 17:33 TLB

If a husband does not understand this principle or does not practice it, not only will his wife be frustrated, but he will soon become discontent and restless in his relationship with her and look for a way out. Husbands often find it difficult to stay in the confines of marriage. The pressures of lust, frustration, aggravation, irritation, discontentment, misalignment, and miscommunication drive against a man's ability to stay. If he listens to his will, he will seek to break out of the boundaries imposed by marriage. It is only if he is willing to submit to and trust the Lord that he will find the strength to commit fully and love his wife.

Self will always say, "If it be Thy will, pass this bitter cup from me."

Self is going to say, "I love her, and her sister."

Self is going to say, "I'm tired of her and I want somebody else."

Self is going to say, "I've been married to her for ten years and I wonder what it would be like to be with somebody new."

Self must be crucified, and that can only occur if we have an intimate relationship with the Lord.

Self says, "I've been reading the Word daily for years. I think I know it by now. I don't need to read it anymore. I'll just meditate on what I already know."

Self says, "I've been praying for this for a long time, but God doesn't answer, so I think I'll just give up on this."

Self says, "God isn't meeting my needs the way I want Him to meet them. I think I'll try another religion."

If we give in to self, we will see a selfish, self-centered attitude permeate every area of our lives, including marriage and church. When people we don't particularly like or with whom we don't agree come into the church, self rises up and says, "If it be Thy will, please tell them to go elsewhere."

Self says, "I'm tired of this pastor and I want to hear somebody new."

Self says, "I've been going to this church for years now. I wonder what it would be like to go to a church down the street that doesn't require so much of me."

Ultimately, the conflict with self always strikes at our relationship with the Lord, and our relationship must be a daily, ongoing conversation. Just as Paul said that loving your wife is an ongoing, continual process, crucifying the flesh and self is not a one-day deal! Paul said in 1 Corinthians 15:31, "I die *daily.*"

You give your life every day, and that takes sacrifice and endurance. Sacrificial love requires daily giving and a lifetime commitment, but you can do it if you trust God and walk in His ways.

Selflessness also takes sheer, gut-wrenching willpower.

A husband's sacrificial love is to be a voluntary act of his will. Husbands are not to wait for their wives to ask or demand their love. God is the one who commands us to love in this way, and sometimes we just don't feel like it, so we have to make ourselves do it. A husband's giving up of self for a wife is not to be the by-product of her constant nagging, whining, or manipulation. Even if she nags, we are to spontaneously give ourselves for her because we are yielding to the will of the Father. And husbands, most likely the nagging will cease when you step up and love her!

No wife should ever demand the love of her husband, just as no husband should ever demand the submission of his wife. Submission is something a wife does "as unto the Lord" (Ephesians 5:22). Loving is something a husband does "even as Christ also loved the church" (Ephesians 5:25). There is no accommodation for rebellion in a wife, and there is no accommodation for anything less than total dying to self in a husband. Crucifixion is not punishment or rebuke or chastisement or torture. It is death! Jesus gave *His life* on the cross. He yielded all of His will to the Father. And He did it so His bride might have her needs met: salvation, redemption, restoration, deliverance, healing, and wholeness.

It is a challenge for a man to be bridled to a marriage! To many men, it becomes a cross because there is something unnatural about being positioned in one place and in one relationship. There is something in the flesh nature of a man that resists being restricted. Does that mean it is difficult for Jesus to love His Church? No. But it was diffi-cult for Jesus to give His life, be crucified, be separated from the Father, and literally go to hell and back to gain His bride. He sweat blood over that decision!

Jesus endured agony and torture and pain in His soul and spirit when He made the decision to yield His will to the Father's. He knew in the Garden of Gethsemane what awaited Him. He saw then that the Father would turn His back on Him. For the first time in eternity past and present, Jesus would know what it meant to be forsaken by the Father. Perhaps this was the greatest horror of all. And yet He exerted His willpower and chose to do the will of His Father.

Husbands, we forget that we have the same ability! We are empowered by the Holy Spirit just as Jesus was in the Garden of Gethsemane. We have His Word to put in our hearts and rule our minds. We have the knowledge that as we obey God's Word and walk in the comfort, direction, and power of the Holy Ghost, we can love our wives as Jesus loves the Church. And we also know there is joy set before us when we obey the Lord in crucifying self and yielding to His plan. There is resurrection!

GETTING CLEANED UP

Husbands, love your wives, even as Christ also loved the church, and gave himself for it.

That he might sanctify and cleanse it with the washing of water by the word.

EPHESIANS 5:25-26

In verse 26, Paul gives us a clear, practical, every-day picture of how the husband loves his wife just as Jesus loves us. He is to sanctify and cleanse his wife, which is to say he is to set her apart from the world and its evil system of thinking and behavior (sanctify) and cleanse her mind and heart of all worldly, devilish thoughts and deeds by speaking the Word of God over her and to her.

What is our Bridegroom doing right now? Jesus is interceding for us before the Father. (See Romans 8:34.) He is praying for us, and as He prays the

Holy Spirit is speaking His words of love, encouragement, wisdom, and power to us. This is the husband's scriptural model to love his wife. He is to pray for her, pray with her, study God's Word for her and with her, and then speak God's Word over her and to her.

To sanctify is to set aside something as being holy. A sanctified vessel is designated for holy purposes or a holy cause. A husband sanctifies his wife as being "set apart" exclusively for God and their marriage relationship. He continually speaks God's words of praise and esteem and value and love over her and to her. The more a husband speaks words of love and value over his wife, the more he cleanses her of any doubt, unbelief, and low self-esteem that she may have. She grows in confidence and faith as he reinforces her identity in Christ and as his special, precious, one-of-a-kind, one-and-only lady.

Husband, tell your wife repeatedly how special she is to you and that you believe she was created just for you. She was fashioned and formed to fit with you, to strengthen you, and to help you. Tell her that you rely on her more than you can express; that other than Jesus, she is the most important person in your life. She is the one with whom you want to share your heart and life. She is the one with whom you want to spend all your days on earth.

One of the reasons a wife is outraged when she discovers her husband has cheated on her is because his promiscuity attempts to defrock her of her self-esteem. She is struck in the face by the fact that she is not exclusive in her exalted position. She feels demeaned and of less value — no longer holy and set apart just for him. She is vulnerable to him because she is submitted to him, and he has allowed another to invade their holy union and tarnish it. He has slung filth and grime on their relationship in the way a vandal defaces a beautiful work of art in a museum. If she is not strong in the Lord, this kind of blow can destroy a wife.

When a husband fails to esteem his wife by speaking and behaving toward her in a way that conveys her value and preciousness, he also erodes her ability to submit to him. He gives her nothing to submit to! And he leaves her uncovered and exposed to the negative, unkind, and injurious remarks others or the devil may speak to her. Again, only a wife who is very grounded and rooted in God can maintain her sense of worth and significance in a marriage where her husband does not know or follow Jesus' example by loving his wife.

Now maybe you are thinking, *My wife is a total mess, a nagging, manipulating, anxiety-ridden, controlling bag of nerves. What's worse, she doesn't have any respect for me and won't listen to a thing I say.* We must remember the shape we were in when Jesus died for us! The Church wasn't the way He wanted the Church to be when He died for us. Jesus died for something that was a mess! You were a mess when you came to Him. Every sinner is a mess when they come to Him.

There are those who seem to think, *I'll get good and then I'll come to God.* It doesn't work that way! Nobody can ever get good enough for God. Nobody can ever cleanse themselves and overcome their own sin nature. We can't change ourselves from the inside out no matter how hard we try or what we try or how long we try. Only God can cleanse the human heart. The psalmist writes,

> I *have cleansed my heart in vain...For all day long have I been plagued, and chastened every morning.*
>
> · PSALM 73:13-14

In other words, "Nothing I do delivers me." The truth of God's Word is that only God delivers, saves, redeems, and cleanses completely. John wrote, "The blood of Jesus Christ his Son cleanseth us from all sin" (1 John 1:7). Throughout God's Word the truth is clear that only God can cleanse the human heart and change our nature. As believers, we are washed as the Word of God continually flows over us with expressions of Jesus' value, esteem, love, concern, and care for us. We grow in confidence and faith as we are washed with expressions of our new identity in Christ Jesus, as His beloved. So if that's true, what does a husband do to model Jesus?

In marriage, the husband devotes himself entirely to his wife. A good husband doesn't take a wife and then keep looking for a better one. A good husband doesn't trade in his wife because she isn't all he desires her to be. Why? Because Jesus doesn't leave us or forsake us or have any less commitment to us because we have a lot of cleaning up to do. He did not find a bride who was just the way He wanted her to be when she became His bride. He has been working on His bride for some two thousand years and He's still working on her to become the bride He desires for Himself.

A good husband doesn't leave his wife just because she disappoints him in some way. He continues to prepare her for the perfection he desires to see in her. You can pray for her to be delivered of the fear that causes her to be anxiety-ridden and to manipulate. You can speak words of love and encouragement over her to assure her that she is loved and highly esteemed. She may look at you like you're from the lunatic asylum for awhile, but eventually, just as Jesus' love always wins our hearts and transforms our lives, your prayers and love will transform her life too.

TALK TO ME!

The fact is, it is up to a husband to teach his wife how to please him. That's what Christ Jesus does for us, His bride. He continually teaches us how to please Him. And how does He teach us? He does it by the Word. He talks to us! The problem many husbands have today in their marriages is a lack of talking. Let me assure you husbands of this: If you don't talk, she won't change! We as believers change as we are taught, understand, and begin to apply the Word to our lives. The Word transforms our minds. Over time, we begin to think, speak, and act as the Lord desires for us to think, speak, and act.

Husbands, talking with your wife doesn't mean that you lay down the law to her, abuse her verbally, or dictate every detail to her as if you are the emperor of the world. It means speaking to her in love. It means speaking in a loving tone of voice and in gentle terms that assure her continually of your love, support, and care. It means speaking out of a motivation of desiring what is best for her and the family — not only what you desire and want and need.

So many wives today have this complaint about their husbands, "I just don't know what he wants!" There's a good reason for that. Their husbands have never told them! Or, they have never said what they want in a loving tone of voice and with a godly purpose. When a wife truly understands what a husband desires and sees that he loves her completely and sacrificially, she is usually eager to respond and quick to do all she can to meet her husband's desires.

Many wives say to their husbands, "I need to talk to you." That's because wives usually need to talk more than husbands feel a need to talk! But what a wife means when she says, "I need to talk," is that she also needs for her husband to listen to her — really hear her — and then talk to her, respond to her. She needs to hear that he loves her, that he understands how she feels, that he longs to meet her needs, and that he recognizes the problems she faces and wants to do something about them. She needs to know what he thinks, decides, feels, and senses, not only for herself but for their children.

The husband who talks to His wife — and who does so often, with love, with openness, and with specificity — is a man who is going to change His wife. If he will change his ways, if he commits to be a godly husband who is rooted in God's Word and is faithful to God's Spirit, what he says to his wife is going to cleanse her. It is going to cause her to separate herself more and more from the evil of the world and the sinful pull of the world. She is going to know how to be his wife, she is going to adore being his wife, and she will have no desire for any other man.

That's the way the Lord cleanses us and washes us. He is always there to have a chat with us! He does it line by line, precept by precept from His Word. He does it by speaking guidance and direction in our hearts. He does it over time, gently, by every means possible. Again and again, He feeds us His Word. He doesn't tell us once what it is that He desires. He tells us again and again, in this story and that, in this lesson and that, in this passage and that, through this experience and that experience. The themes of God's desire run from cover to cover in God's Word and jump into our daily living.

A TIP FOR WIVES

When a husband talks to his wife, it is extremely important in those times that she listen. That is part of a submissive spirit. Many women do not seem to know how difficult it is for a man to trust a woman with his heart. A man can give his body to almost anybody, but he's very particular about where he gives his heart. The trust that a man feels about matters of the heart is so fragile that it can be destroyed in an instant by one insensitive comment or response. When that happens, a man tends to withdraw into himself like a turtle, harbor the hurt that he feels, and become even more reluctant to open up in the future.

When a husband opens up to his wife and discusses how he feels about something, what he dreams of doing, his vision for his own life and the life of your family...listen to what he is saying. Hear him out fully. Listen with your heart. Don't interrupt. Don't move in to fill a silence that might occur for a few seconds or even minutes. The more your husband is allowed to articulate to you the vision he has for your family, the faith he has in the Lord, and the desires he has for you as a couple in the Lord...the more secure you are going to feel in your marriage and the more confident and valuable you are going to feel as a wife.

DEMONSTRATING JESUS

Both the husband and wife are deeply challenged. It is no less difficult for a husband to love his wife, and to do so in a genuinely sacrificial way, than it is for a wife to submit to and reverence her husband. We know that no wife will ever submit perfectly, nor will any husband love with perfect sacrificial love. Nevertheless, Paul sets these goals because the reality is that Jesus is the authority over the Church and He loves the Church with perfect sacrificial love. Again, as the wife models submission to Jesus to the world, the husband models the love of Jesus to the world. Natural marriage models spiritual marriage of Jesus and the Church.

The wife is to submit to her husband as the Church is to submit to the Lord.

The husband is to love his wife as Christ loved the Church.

This model requires a great deal of mutuality! I believe a husband finds it much easier to love his wife as Christ loved the Church if his wife submits to him and to Christ. Likewise, a wife finds it much easier to submit to her husband if he loves her with a sacrificial love and continually seeks to cherish her and nourish her. However, husband, whether she is submitting to you or not, the Word of God commands you to love her. You are fulfilling Jesus' role to show the mystery of the Church to the world, and Jesus' part of the equation is never in question. He never ceases to be the head of the Church. He never ceases to be responsible to God the Father for the body of Christ. He never ceases to love His bride and to offer Himself for her completely.

When loving your wife gets tough — and it will get tough — remember the joy set before you. First Peter 3:7 says that if you do this, your prayers will be unhindered! And even if your wife digs in her heels and never submits to you, you are making the most powerful statement to her, your children, your neighbors, your church, and your associates at work: Jesus is our loving, saving, healing, and delivering Lord!

6

AS HE LOVES HIMSELF

Did you know that Jesus loves Himself? Think about this for one moment. Never in the Word of God does Jesus put Himself down. Never does He insult Himself, make a joke at His own expense, or complain that He is nothing but a worm. Does that mean that Jesus was arrogant and prideful? We know that's not true! But Jesus knew who He was and had a healthy, godly love for Himself. This is revealed most vividly in this astounding statement of the apostle Paul's in his letter to the Philippians:

Let this mind be in you, which was also in Christ Jesus:

Who, being in the form of God, thought it not robbery to be equal with God:

But made himself of no reputation, and took upon him the form of a servant, and was made in the likeness of men:

And being found in fashion as a man, he humbled himself, and became obedient unto death, even the death of the cross.

PHILIPPIANS 2:5-8

We are going to zero in on one phrase in verse 6: Jesus didn't think He was robbing God to be equal with Him, and His reaction to this fact motivated Him to humble Himself to the point of death. This seems impossible to our natural way of thinking. How can being equal with God motivate someone to humble themselves? Wouldn't being equal with God cause us to get puffed up with pride and arrogance?

Husbands, when you really know who you are in Christ, when you begin to get a glimpse of all God has done for you in Christ Jesus, when you allow Him to bless you with all spiritual blessings in Christ Jesus, and when you feel the waves of His love and acceptance in the beloved move through your heart and soul, you are going to fall on your face in humility and lay down your life! Knowing all this is what forms the foundation of loving yourself, which is then the motivation for loving others. When we understand and receive His love for us, our first response is to love as He loves.

We can see from Jesus' example that there is a godly love for ourselves that is essential to loving as God loves. The kind of love I'm talking about says what God says about us and thinks what God thinks about us. Because Jesus understood and experienced the love and acceptance of His Father,

He desired only to please Him. And the way to please God is to love what He loves.

NOURISH AND CHERISH

A married couple needs to understand that when they speak to their spouse, they are actually speaking to themselves. Two have become one. What you say to your spouse has a direct reflection on you. Furthermore, what you say to your spouse indicates how you feel about *yourself*.

> **S**o ought men to love their wives as their own bodies. He that loveth his wife loveth himself.
>
> EPHESIANS 5:28

Through the years I have counseled numerous couples, among them couples in which the husbands have beaten their wives. In every encounter I've ever had with a wife-beater, I have found the wife-beater to be a man who didn't like himself. He had extremely low self-esteem. He had something in his past that he had not forgiven himself for, and he was angry and disappointed in himself.

When husbands approach their wives, they act out how they feel about themselves. Husband, if you don't know how you feel about yourself, take a close look at the way you treat your wife. The Bible tells us clearly, the degree to which you love your wife, you love yourself.

If you treat your wife with disrespect or anger or abusive behavior, you need to know two things: God commands you to break this pattern of behavior, and He will not reward you as long as you act that way toward your wife. That is why Peter wrote that a man must care for his wife or his prayers will be hindered. (See 1 Peter 3:7.) When a husband acts in anger toward his wife and fails to model Jesus to her, many of the promises that would otherwise have been fulfilled in his life are hindered. But how does this work? And what, specifically, are we to do?

> *No man ever yet hated his own flesh, but nourisheth and cherisheth it, even as the Lord the church.*
>
> EPHESIANS 5:29

The Greek words translated "nourisheth" and "cherisheth" provide tremendous keys to the revelation the Holy Spirit gives to husbands in these verses in Ephesians. First, "nourisheth" is the word *ektrepho*, which means to educate and train in the way a teacher educates and trains a student. This is very easy to see in our Lord and Savior, who gave us the Holy Spirit to lead us into all truth, remind us of His words, and even tell us things to come. But it is a sad commentary on the Church that so many men are more like the spiritual babies of their homes than the spiritual teachers of their homes. It's time for men to rise up and take their places as the spiritual heads of their households, to study God's Word and live God's Word before their wives, children, business associates, and neighbors.

Second, we have the word "cherisheth," the Greek word *thalpo*, which means to brood over in the same way a mother hen will brood over her chicks or the Holy Spirit brooded over the earth and brought it to life in Genesis 1. This is a life-giving, Spirit-breathing word! And when we put these two words together, we see a husband who imparts the living Word to his wife, who prays over her in the Spirit, who walks in the ways of God, and loves his wife as he loves himself.

If the first man, Adam, had nourished Eve, rather than allowing Eve to nourish him, the fall never would have happened. Adam and Eve broke the divine order when the "nourishee" became the "nourisher." Eve gave to Adam when he should have been giving to her. Adam gave place to the devil when he failed to give Eve the nourishment she needed. Because Adam didn't nourish her with God's Word, the devil came in to nourish her with a lie.

It is a husband's responsibility to build up his wife on the inside. The only thing that will give her confidence, courage, purpose, value, and significance is the Word and anointing of God. Obviously, Adam didn't tell Eve everything she needed to know because she told the serpent that God had said they shouldn't "touch" the tree of the knowledge of good and evil. (See Genesis 3:3.) From this example, husbands, we can see how vital it is for us to provide those things that our wives need for growth, development, and vibrant spiritual life — not only food, shelter, and clothing, but the things that feed her spirit.

So many wives today are trying to drag their husbands to church, seminars, and retreats so they can grow in the Lord. Where are the men who are leading their wives to church and seminars and retreats? So many wives are trying to get their husbands interested in spiritual matters, to read their Bibles and listen to sound teaching of God's principles. Where are the men who are leading their wives to sources that will nourish their spirits?

It's time men faced up to this role in marriage and started patterning their lives and their marriages according to God's Word, not according to the way the world operates. Our role model is Jesus Christ and the manual for life and marriage is His Word. Ephesians 5:29 says that we are to nourish and cherish our wives "even as the Lord the church." The Lord continually tells His people who they are in Him. They are His beloved children, His people, His delight. He continually feeds His people the revelation of His Word so that He might nourish them and cause them to grow up into His image. And the Holy Spirit broods over us, bearing witness with our spirit that we are God's child, that we are loved, that we are cherished by our Bridegroom.

SERVE, MINISTER, HARVEST

Knowing who we are in Christ Jesus, husbands, means we know we have been made the heads of our homes. We have been empowered and anointed to fill that position. But God not only gives the husband power; He always gives purpose for that power. There is always a vision, a dream, a high calling in Christ Jesus set before us. And in our marriages, the high calling is loving and serving our wives.

If a husband sees only his authority and exercises only his power, his wife is going to be miserable and will find it increasingly difficult to submit. Power without purpose becomes reckless and dangerous. If a husband, however, gets the full picture that his power is for the purpose of serving, he will not abuse his power. His wife will be fulfilled and so will he. There is a level of truth to the saying, "When Mama's happy, everybody's happy"!

The Lord Jesus always linked authority with servanthood. He exemplified this to His disciples at the Last Supper when He rose from the table, laid aside His outer garments, girded Himself with a towel, poured water into a basin, and began to wash the disciples' feet. After He washed their feet, He said:

> **K**now ye what I have done to you?
>
> Ye call me Master and Lord: and ye say well; for so I am.
>
> If I then, your Lord and Master, have washed your feet; ye also ought to wash one another's feet.
>
> For I have given you an example, that ye should do as I have done to you.
>
> Verily, verily, I say unto you, The servant is not greater than his lord; neither he that is sent greater than he that sent him.
>
> If ye know these things, happy are ye if ye do them.
>
> JOHN 13:12-17

You may love your wife and she submits to that love, but then her submission should not be met with domination, but by ministry. Any person who is called to a position of authority in Christ Jesus must lay down their life and become a great servant. When a man marries, his wife becomes his ministry — his number-one ministry. He has responsibility for nourishing and cherishing her far more than he has responsibility for any other person or group of people.

I wrote a song titled "You Are My Ministry" and it is about the relationship between a husband and wife. The lyrics include these lines:

When I think about loving myself,
I think about loving you.
You are my "do me right,"
A special song in the night,
A spiritual part of me,
You are my ministry.

The ministry of the husband to the wife is a ministry of putting her needs before his own needs. Her submission is in all areas of authority; his ministry is in all areas of provision, material and financial as well as emotional and spiritual. The godly husband lives to serve his wife. Being head of his wife means God has given the husband the honor and privilege of taking care of a precious treasure, one of His children. The wife truly belongs to God, and He has entrusted the husband with the responsibility to nourish and cherish her, to impart God's life and Word into her. And when you are given the responsibility to grow and develop something, you get a harvest.

When a man takes a wife to himself, he takes her into his total life. She becomes a part of him and he becomes a part of her. They are one. For example, if the husband is a workaholic, the wife will live in a hurricane of work and pressure and stress. If he is not whole in Christ Jesus, she is going to be the recipient of the way he expresses all those areas of brokenness. Whatever he is, she will enter fully into his cycles, his systems, his self-esteem, his restlessness, his peace, his degree of wholeness. What he sows into her life will bring forth a harvest from her.

A wife produces a harvest from what her husband sows into her life. She has the capacity to multiply what he says and does, to bring forth a harvest from his seed. We see this in the physical realm when a man sows seed into her womb and she produces the harvest of a child. We see this in the emotional realm when a man sows anger into his wife and she produces a harvest of anger, distrust, and rejection. And it is the husband who reaps that harvest. What he sows into his wife will be the harvest he reaps from his marriage.

Thank God Jesus sows wholeness, peace, joy, and love into us through His Word and by His presence. His divine seed produces an eternal harvest in us. And it is Jesus who will reap back that harvest. He is sowing into a Church who will become a "glorious bride" without spot, wrinkle, or blemish. But the production of a good harvest is not always automatic.

The challenge to every wife is to produce a good harvest when good seed is planted into her. She must guard her own heart and make sure that she has not hardened it to her husband or to God. She must ask the Lord continually to keep her fruitful and fertile so that she has the ability to produce a good harvest from good seed, to be the good ground Jesus talks about in Mark 4:20.

EMPOWERMENT

So ought men to love their wives as their own bodies. He that loveth his wife loveth himself.

For no man ever yet hated his own flesh; but nourisheth and cherisheth it, even as the Lord the church:

For we are members of his body, of his flesh, and of his bones.

EPHESIANS 5:28-30

We are now coming to the end of Paul's discussion about the husband's role in marriage, which is a mirror reflection of Jesus' role as Bridegroom to the Church. It is obvious that our union with Christ Jesus as our Lord is not a union that is only for Sundays, when we are talking about religion, or when we are thinking spiritual thoughts. Our union with Christ Jesus makes us one with Him in every area of our lives at all times and in all situations because we are members of His body, even of His flesh and bones. We are Jesus in this earth!

His will should be our will.

His passion should be our passion.

His compassion should be our compassion.

His blessing and honor and power and glory should radiate from our countenance and demonstrate His person to every person we encounter.

As husbands, this is no small task! (Now who feels like they've been run through the washing machine?!) But men, we must remember that God has not left us without assistance. He has empowered us with everything we need to succeed. We have His Word. We have His Spirit. We have His name. We have His wisdom. We have His love. And He has not only appointed us, but He has anointed us to be Jesus to our wives and show forth Jesus to the world.

For this cause shall a man leave his father and mother, and shall be joined unto his wife, and they two shall be one flesh.

This is a great mystery: but I speak concerning Christ and the church.

Nevertheless let every one of you in particular so love his wife even as himself; and the wife see that she reverence her husband.

EPHESIANS 5:31-33

In this final section of Ephesians 5, Paul says that although he has been speaking in practical terms about marriage between a man and woman, he has really been talking about the Church's relationship with Jesus Christ, which is a mystery. The issue is not marriage; the issue is the mystery. Marriage between a husband and wife is merely the illustration of the mystery, which is the marriage of Jesus and the Church, the relationship of the Head and His body, the Bridegroom and the bride.

In light of this truth, God's infinite wisdom and mercy have established the marriage relationship so that we can only accomplish it by walking hand in hand and face to face with Him. The degree to which we pursue intimacy with our heavenly Bridegroom is the degree to which we will enjoy wedded bliss with our spouse on the earth. And every aspect of our earthly union reflects the divine design and ecstasy of our heavenly union with Christ Jesus. For example, before we entered into covenant with Him, Jesus was the aggressor. He was wooing us, pursuing us, chasing us down, and courting us. But it is also interesting to note that He was rejected by another before He sought our hearts:

> He was in the world, and the world was made by him, and the world knew him not.
> He came unto his own, and his own received him not.
>
> JOHN 1:10-11

Jesus became flesh and dwelt among us, but when the time came for Him to take a bride, instead of reaching for an earthly bride, He reached for a spiritual bride — Israel. But Israel rejected Him and, like the first Adam, there was no helpmeet for Him. So He went to the cross, God opened up His side, and out poured the blood which would bring forth His spiritual bride. That is why the cross is referred to as Jesus' *passion*.

When Jesus burst forth from the tomb He began to build His bride just as Eve had been built for Adam. You see, in the Hebrew language of the Old Testament, it says that Adam was created and formed, but Eve was *built*. (See Genesis 2:7,22.) So it was no coincidence that Jesus declared that He would *build* His Church:

> He saith unto them, But whom say ye that I am?
>
> And Simon Peter answered and said, Thou art the Christ, the Son of the living God.
>
> And Jesus answered and said unto him, Blessed art thou, Simon Barjona: for flesh and blood hath not revealed it unto thee, but my Father which is in heaven.
>
> And I say also unto thee, That thou art Peter, and upon this rock I will build my church; and the gates of hell shall not prevail against it.
>
> MATTHEW 16:15-18

The Church is a spiritual bride which is built upon the revelation knowledge of who Jesus Christ is. Jesus gave His life for us, and like a blushing bride who glows with adoration for her bridegroom, we should walk in the glory of the Lord. We are one with Him. We are bone of His bone and flesh of His flesh, members of His body, and walk in the light as He is in the light.

THE HOLY HUNT

For this cause shall a man leave his father and mother....

EPHESIANS 5:31

Jesus had to leave His Father in heaven to come to us and become one with us, and a man must leave his mother and father to become one with his wife. But we must also leave. The Church must leave the world which gave us physical birth to be spiritually joined with our Lord and Savior Jesus Christ. Ultimately, at the resurrection, we will also be physically joined with Him.

In marriage, it is the man's role to come to the place in his maturity and in his walk with the Lord that he says, "It's time I leave mother and father and establish a home of my own. It's time I find a wife." And then, the hunting instinct takes over. The godly man will rely on the Lord to lead him to the person who is right for him, but he is always the aggressor just as Jesus is the aggressor.

Although for hundreds of years the vast majority of men on the earth have not fed their families by hunting wild animals, men are still hunters on the inside. A single woman, on the other hand, is the game. She simply goes about her life in purity and holiness before the Lord knowing that when God gets ready to bring a husband to her, it will be at the right time. A single woman doesn't need to do anything to put herself in a man's way or pursue him. He's supposed to find her and win her heart.

This certainly doesn't mean that women are to be victims of stalkers! It simply means that scouting out a man is not the role of a godly woman. A single woman can pray for God to send the husband of His choice in His timing and for His purposes, but she needs to be about those things that the Lord puts in her heart to do. She doesn't need to go out and run down and tackle a man.

This also does not mean that a Christian woman should accept the first hunter who finds her! She must accept the one she has peace in her heart about, the one she knows God has prepared her for, the one she will joyfully submit to for the rest of her life — and the one who has been prepared by God to love, nourish, and cherish her.

God didn't bring Eve on the scene until the stage was set and Adam was in place to care for her and love her. He didn't birth the Church into being until the stage was set and Jesus Christ was the resurrected Lord, risen to care for her and love her and nourish her. So women, don't say yes to a man who hasn't submitted himself fully to the Lord. Wait until the stage is properly set for you!

In terms of the mystery, Jesus is always on the hunt for His bride. He was on the hunt for us long before we even knew His name or knew anything about Him. He searches continually for those who will turn away from sin and believe in Him. He searches continually for human hearts who desire to know Him with greater intimacy and are willing to do whatever He tells them to do. Jesus is the hunter of the human heart.

Now a word of caution: There is also a supernatural stalker who is after us, and his name is Satan. He is described as our adversary who operates as a "roaring lion, seeking whom he may devour" (1 Peter 5:8). Jesus said that the devil comes only "to steal, and to kill, and to destroy" (John 10:10). The devil is looking for trophies to hang on his wall. He is looking for people he might destroy forever. He tortures his prey and inflicts as much pain and agony as possible before he moves in for the final kill.

In sharp contrast, Jesus searches for us so that He might give us life "and that more abundantly" (John 10:10). He seeks us out with all grace and mercy so that we might inherit "eternal glory by Christ Jesus" and that He might "perfect, stablish, strengthen, and settle" us (1 Peter 5:10). If we develop an intimate relationship with Jesus, if we allow this holy hunter to capture our hearts and minds and fill us with His love and light, we will not fall for the dark lies and deception of the devil.

HOLY AFFECTION

> *For this cause shall a man leave his father and mother, and shall be joined unto his wife, and they two shall be one flesh.*
>
> EPHESIANS 5:31

After a man has left his mother and father, has found his wife, and she has accepted him as the husband God has for her, they are joined together. They are to be so joined together that they are one. Now we do not have to have a doctorate degree to understand that when we are joined together with another person we *touch* one another! Affection is holy. It is sacred. And it is something which God ordained between a husband and wife to reflect and illustrate the intimacy Jesus desires with His bride. Furthermore, if affection is not practiced, the covenant becomes very hard to honor.

A number of years ago, an experiment was conducted which tested this very principle. A clinical psychologist was seeking to discover the effects of touch on the pituitary glands and the growth glands in the body. Two groups of babies and nurses were part of the study. One group of nurses was told only to take care of the biological needs of the babies. They were to feed the babies and change their diapers, but not to touch them or hold them. The other group of nurses was told to handle their babies with a great deal of affection. In addition to feeding their babies and changing their diapers, they were to touch them, massage them, hold them, and cuddle them.

Both groups of babies were observed over time and the clinical psychologist was able to chart measurable differences in the two groups. The babies who had not been touched or massaged were dwarfed. They failed to develop normally and to thrive and grow to their potential. The study pointed to the conclusion that affection enhances and promotes good health and normal growth.[1]

Affection is also one of the barometers of a healthy marriage. An intimate relationship always involves touch. It is normal for a husband and wife to desire to touch each other, to hold hands, to hug and kiss, to caress each other. Show me a couple who doesn't touch very much and I'll show you a marriage that is in trouble. Now I'm not just referring to sex

---

[1] Anna Nidecker, "Maternal Depravation Redness Cortisol Levels," Medscope. Webpage accessed 1/16/99. http://women-shealth.medscope.com/IMNB/Pediatric News/1998/v.32.n01/pn3201.10.01.htm/

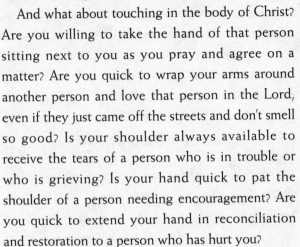

alone, but to affection — of skin touching skin and bodies touching bodies even with clothes on.

And what about touching in the body of Christ? Are you willing to take the hand of that person sitting next to you as you pray and agree on a matter? Are you quick to wrap your arms around another person and love that person in the Lord, even if they just came off the streets and don't smell so good? Is your shoulder always available to receive the tears of a person who is in trouble or who is grieving? Is your hand quick to pat the shoulder of a person needing encouragement? Are you quick to extend your hand in reconciliation and restoration to a person who has hurt you?

There is nothing as chilling as an icy touch or an empty embrace. Nothing produces loneliness like false intimacy. And God knows this! He is a Father who loves to embrace and touch His children, and He loves for us to come running into His arms. It grieves Him when we turn from Him and resist His affection, and when we resist receiving His divine touch, we destroy our own ability to express affection and concern for others.

Our affection toward one another must be innocent, pure, and genuine. There is no room for hypocrisy in this! There is no place for manipulation or insincerity. If we are to be "fitly joined" together as husbands and wives and as members of the body of Christ, we must submit and love with heartfelt affection. And the only way for us to express genuine affection is to receive it first from heaven. The way we do that is to stay in communion with God, not just in service at church, but every moment of the day and night.

HOLY COMMUNION

The bride of Christ was birthed from the blood which flowed from Jesus' side on the cross, and we are forever united in spirit in Him. Yet we are separate in space and in physical form from Him. It is a mystery. We experience intimacy with Jesus in worship, in holy communion with Him. It is in the Holy of Holies in the spirit realm that our spirit and His Spirit realize oneness, where we are fully activated and fully fused and fully of one accord. Worship is the consummation of our relationship with the Lord. A wedding is not fully complete until the union is consummated, and a marriage has no substance without regular intimacy. Our wedding with the Lord is not fully complete until we worship Him as Lord and Savior, and our marriage to Him is only alive and vibrant if we continue to be a worshipper of our Lord.

Nothing is as exhilarating in a marriage as a good sexual relationship. Other things may be as important or as good, but nothing is as euphoric, powerful, passionate, or explosive. And nothing has the same ability to create. In the same manner, our special times of communion with the Lord are the most exhilarating, euphoric, passionate, powerful, and explosive times of our lives. And nothing we do in the church has the same ability to bring forth the harvest of souls He longs for.

We cannot enter into holy communion with the Lord without yielding self completely. In worship, self becomes totally unimportant. The only thing that matters is God. What He desires, what He commands, and just what He is totally consumes us. We lose ourselves in His presence, and we do so willingly. It's hard to imagine that anyone could remain puffed up in God's awesome presence. He is everything!

When we lay aside self and love God with all our heart, soul, mind, and strength, He fills us with His presence. Whatever we yield to Him, He occupies. All the areas of our lives that we give to Him, He moves into them with all the fruit of the Spirit we need to love and minister and all the gifts we need to do what He's called us to do. Why? Because He inhabits the praises of His people. He moves in where He is welcome and then He redecorates! When we live in a perpetual state and lifestyle of holy communion, everything we touch is blessed and beautified by God.

HOLY AND GLORIOUS

When a husband and wife become one flesh, it is both reproductive and redemptive. Not only do they produce children, but they produce intimacy with one another that restores and completes and makes whole. Likewise, when the bride of Christ becomes one with her Bridegroom and receives the seed of His Word, intimacy with Christ Jesus restores us, completes us, and makes us whole, and babies are born into the kingdom of God.

The foremost thing that is birthed out of worshipping Jesus Christ is souls. Unbelievers who find themselves caught up in the worship of a body of believers find themselves drawn to God in ways they have never felt drawn before. They long for the joy and reconciliation, forgiveness and healing, and total freedom and deliverance they see all around them in worshipping believers.

In addition to souls, we come to the place Ephesians 5:27 describes:

> That he might present it to himself a glorious church, not having spot, or wrinkle, or any such thing; but that it should be holy and without blemish.

Jesus makes us glorious!

The blessing He bestows upon His bride is a blessing that makes us the envy of all who see us. It is a blessing that not only nourishes us and beautifies us, but which transforms us into a kingdom of priests unto our God. Nevertheless, it comes with a great price. God is using *our house* to preach to our community, and this responsibility causes our knees to buckle!

Who we are at home cuts to the very gut and root of who we really are. Yet this passage in Ephesians is telling us we must be yielded to the Word and the Spirit to the point that our private lives are open for public scrutiny. That makes us very vulnerable. If He just wants to use us from nine to five during the day, we can do that. If He wants to use us from six to nine in the evening for a service, we're available. But if we are to understand that our *whole life* is the canvas on which He paints the glorious Gospel, then we are intimidated! Most of us feel too weak to be under the world's microscope twenty-four hours a day, seven days a week.

Nevertheless, that's what Paul is saying. The most intimate relationship we experience on earth is what God has chosen to illustrate His relationship with His Church. He has typecast each of us to play a role in His drama (more often a comedy!)

without our permission and has challenged us to be conformed into His image. We are not Him, and yet we must put Him on and play Him. (And the Word of God assures husbands that the better we play Him, the better He will answer our prayers!)

Any actor will tell you that when you play a role on the stage, you cannot break character. That means you must exhibit the personality and character of the person you are playing at all times and without exception. Thus, we cannot break character; we are bound to exhibit the personality and character of Jesus Christ at all times, in all situations, and with all people.

We are His people and He is our God!

We walk in His glory and emanate His presence!

We become His expression of power and majesty!

We are His resplendent jewel on the earth!

We are the demonstration of His love and the illustration of His redemptive work to every life we touch!

Oh, what a wonder and a marvel to know that the King of Kings and Lord of Lords has chosen us to be His own and we are wedded to Him for all eternity!

REFERENCES

Adam Clarke Commentary. 6 vols. Adam Clarke. *PC Study Bible.* Version 2.1J. CD-ROM. Seattle: Biblesoft, 1993-1998.

Barnes' Notes on the OT & NT. 14 vols. Albert Barnes. *PC Study Bible.* Version 2.1J. CD-ROM. Seattle: Biblesoft, 1993-1998.

The Bible Knowledge Commentary: An Exposition of the Scriptures. Dallas Seminary faculty. Editors, John F. Walvoord, Roy B. Zuck. Wheaton, IL: Victor Books. 1983-1985. Published in electronic form by Logos Research Systems Inc., 1996.

Brown, Driver, & Briggs' Definitions. Francis Brown, D.D., D. Litt., S. R. Driver, D.D., D. Litt., and Charles A. Briggs, D.D., D. Litt. *PC Study Bible.* Version 2.1J. CD-ROM. Seattle: Biblesoft, 1993-1998.

Expositor's Bible Commentary, New Testament. Frank E. Gaebelein, General Editor. J. D. Douglas, Associate Editor. Grand Rapids, MI: Zondervan Publishing House, 1976-1992.

A Greek-English Lexicon of the New Testament and Other Early Christian Literature. Walter Bauer. Second edition, revised and augmented by F. W. Gingrich, Fredrick Danker from Walter Bauer's fifth edition. Chicago and London: The University of Chicago Press, 1958.

The Greek New Testament. Editor Kurt Aland, et al. CD-ROM of the 3rd edition, corrected. Federal Republic of Germany: United Bible Societies, 1983. Published in electronic form by Logos Research Systems, Inc. 1996.

Greek (UBS) text and Hebrew (BHS) text. PC Study Bible. Version 2.1J. CD-ROM. Seattle: Biblesoft, 1993-1998.

The Hebrew-Greek Key Study Bible. Compiled and edited by Spiros Zodhiates, Th.D. World Bible Publishers, Inc., 1984, 1991.

Interlinear Bible. PC Study Bible. Version 2.1J. CD-ROM Seattle: Biblesoft, 1993-1998.

Jamieson, Fausset & Brown Commentary. 6 vols. Robert Jamieson, A. R. Fausset, and David Brown. *PC Study Bible.* Version 2.1J. CD-ROM. Seattle: Biblesoft, 1993-1998.

A Manual Grammar of the Greek New Testament. H. E. Dana, Th.D. and Julius R. Mantey. Toronto, Canada: MacMillan Publishing Company, 1927.

Matthew Henry's Commentary. 6 vols. Matthew Henry. *PC Study Bible.* Version 2.1J. CD-ROM. Seattle: Biblesoft, 1993-1998.

The New Linguistic and Exegetical Key to the Greek New Testament. Fritz Reineker, Revised version by Cleon Rogers and Cleon Rogers III. Grand Rapids, MI: Zondervan Publishing Company, 1998.

Strong's Exhaustive Concordance of the Bible. J. B. Strong. *PC Study Bible.* Version 2.1J. CD-ROM. Seattle: Biblesoft, 1993-1998.

Vincent's Word Studies in the NT. 4 vols. Marvin R. Vincent, D.D. *PC Study Bible.* Version 2.1J. CD-ROM. Seattle: Biblesoft, 1993-1998.

Wuest's Word Studies from the Greek New Testament for the English Reader. Volume One, Ephesians. Kenneth S. Wuest. Grand Rapids, MI: Wm. B. Eerdmans Publishing Company, 1953.

ABOUT THE AUTHOR

T. D. Jakes is the founder and senior pastor of The Potter's House church in Dallas, Texas. A highly celebrated author with several best-selling books to his credit, he frequently ministers in massive crusades and conferences across the nation. His weekly television broadcast is viewed nationally in millions of homes. Bishop Jakes lives in Dallas with his wife, Serita, and their five children.

To contact T. D. Jakes, write:
T. D. Jakes Ministries
International Communications Center
P. O. Box 210887
Dallas, Texas 75211

or visit his website at:
www.tdjakes.org

Loose That Man and Let Him Go!

(special gift edition)

Just for Men!

Includes 64 inspiring and motivational devotions written specifically for men. The perfect gift for any man—any time of the year.
AP-086
$16.99

Woman Thou Art Loosed

(special gift edition)

Great "anytime" gift for any woman!

The bestselling devotional, now in an exquisite cloth-bound gift edition! Daily devotions developed from the bestselling book by T. D. Jakes. The perfect gift for every woman, this cherished volume of hope and expectancy will be treasured and lovingly passed on for generations to come.
AP-085
$16.99

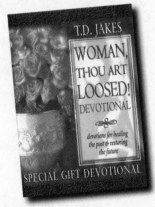

Six Pillars for the Believer *(video 1)*

First in the Series

In chapter one of Ephesians, The Apostle Paul helps us discover who we are, whose we are, what we have, and how to receive all the spiritual blessings that God has prepared for us as His children.
AP-146
$19.99

Six Pillars for the Believer *(video 2)*

Second in the Series

In chapter two of Ephesians, The Apostle Paul teaches us about our resurrection out of sin and death and how we can learn to walk with Christ in fullness of joy. Bishop Jakes encourages us to help others receive the wealth and blessing of God.
AP-147
$19.99

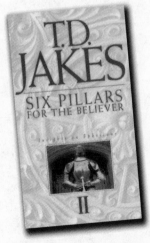

Six Pillars for the Believer *(video 3)*

Third in the Series

In chapter three of Ephesians, Paul gives us a brief autobiography. We learn in this chapter that Paul considers himself a slave for Christ. Bishop Jakes gives tremendous insight into Paul's background and holds him up as an example of forsaking self and focusing on Christ.

AP-148
$19.99

Six Pillars for the Believer *(video 4)*

Fourth in the Series

In chapter four of Ephesians, Paul shows us how to pursue the calling that God has for each of us, and he motivates us to move on to the next level. Bishop Jakes exhorts us, saying our walk as believers should be a divine reflection of our unique calling.

AP-149
$19.99

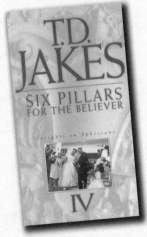

Six Pillars for the Believer *(video 5)*

Fifth in the Series

In chapter five of Ephesians, Paul challenges us to not just walk in love, but to follow Christ's example and love others just as He loved us. Bishop Jakes points out that Paul's desire was for Christians to demonstrate outwardly what God had done inwardly.
AP-150
$19.99

Six Pillars for the Believer *(video 6)*

Sixth in the Series

In chapter six of Ephesians, Paul deals with our relationships with others and how we are to submit ourselves to God and to others. Bishop Jakes speaks in depth on God's desire concerning how we manage our own house and gives several powerful principles for parents.
AP-151
$19.99

T.D. Jakes Speaks to Men

Power-Packed Quotes for Men

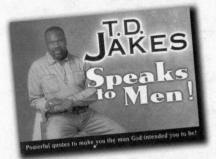

T.D. Jakes' portable for men is packed with motivational, inspiring, and dynamic quotes. Each page contains a quote taken from one of Bishop Jakes' liberating video series.
AP-986
$6.99

T.D. Jakes Speaks to Women

Life-Changing Quotes for Women

As you read each quote in this inspirational portable, you will be challenged, comforted, healed, and set free! Bishop Jakes' message is clear—that no matter where you have been or what you have done, God has forgiven you and wants to heal your past so you can change your future.
AP-987
$6.99

Lay Aside the Weight

T.D. Jakes shares the way to a new you!

Discover the same nutritional, weight-loss secrets and discipline techniques that Bishop Jakes incorporated into his life. Take control! Using the five steps outlined in this dynamic book, you will learn how to shed unwanted weight in every area of your life. Includes a complete section of weight-fighting recipes!
AP-035
$19.99

Lay Aside the Weight

(workbook & journal)

Step by Step!

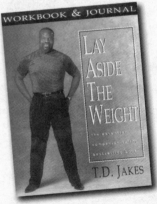

The best way to get the most out of T.D. Jakes' bestselling book, *Lay Aside the Weight*, is to make it applicable to your own life. Now it's even easier to do just that! This extensive workbook and journal enables you to focus on the specific health information you need to be completely successful in your health and weight-loss plan.
AP-083
$11.99

Woman Thou Art Loosed

The One That Started it All!

This book has changed hundreds of thousands of women and continues to grow in popularity. This beautiful hardcover edition makes a great gift for a loved one, friend, or even you!
AP-985
$19.99

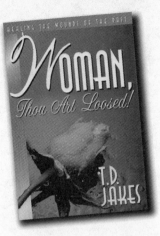

Woman, Thou Art Loosed! *(devotional)*

Bestseller now a Devotional

This insightful devotional was created for the thousands of women from around the world that have received healing and restoration through the *Woman, Thou Art Loosed!* message. Each liberating chapter is designed to assist you in keeping the binding chains of the past from refastening themselves in your life.
AP-020
$13.99

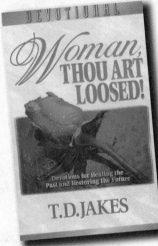

So You Call Yourself a Man?

Bestselling Devotional for Men

Written in the charismatic style that T.D. Jakes is know for, this devotional for men continues to be a bestseller year after year. Be challenged through the lives of ordinary men in the Bible who became extraordinary, and let God use your life to accomplish extraordinary things.

AP-026
$12.99

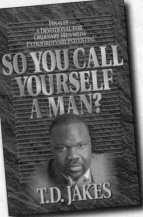

Loose that Man & Let Him Go! *(paperback)*

Over 250,000 sold!

Within the pages of this book begins the healing of fathers and sons. God's Word will release the empty, nagging ache of unresolved conflicts, and men will learn how to turn their pressures into power as they bask in the revelation light of God's plan.

AP-915
$13.99

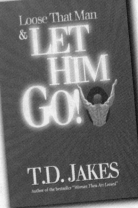

Additional copies of this book and other book titles
from ALBURY PUBLISHING are
available at your local bookstore.

ALBURY PUBLISHING
P. O. Box 470406
Tulsa, Oklahoma 74147-0406

For a complete list of our titles,
visit us at our website:
www.alburypublishing.com

For international and Canadian orders,
please contact:

Access Sales International
2448 East 81st Street
Suite 4900
Tulsa, Oklahoma 74137
Phone 918-523-5590   Fax 918-496-2822